SOUTHWEST STYLE

SOUTHWEST STYLE
A Home-Lover's Guide to Architecture and Design

By Linda Mason Hunter
Photography by Peter Vitale

NORTHLAND PUBLISHING

The text type was set in Weiss Roman
The display type was set in Rotis
Composed in the United States of America
Art Director: David Jenney
Designer: Julie Sullivan, Sullivan Santamaria Design, Inc.
Production Assistant: Joan Carstensen, Sullivan Santamaria Design, Inc.

Editor: Brad Melton
Book Editor: Stephanie Bucholz
Photographer: Peter Vitale
Production Supervisor: Lisa Brownfield
Editorial Assistant: Kimberly Fox

Printed in Hong Kong by Midas Printing Limited

CREDITS
All photographs by Peter Vitale unless stated below.
Special thanks to *Veranda* magazine.

CHAPTER ONE
Page 3: Photo by Gene Balzer.
Page 7: Photo courtesy of U.S. Government.
Page 8: Top photo: courtesy of Mesa Verde National Park. Bottom photo: Edward S. Curtis Collection, NAU.PH93.38.31; courtesy of Cline Library, Northern Arizona University.
Page 9: Photo by Geriant Smith.
Page 10–11: Photo by Gene Balzer.

CHAPTER TWO
Page 14: Photo by Gene Balzer.
Page 17: Photo by Richard Levine, New Mexico Earth Adobe, Albuquerque, NM.
Page 19: Photograph by Robert Reck.
Page 22: Photo by Scott S. Warren.
Page 23: Design by Tod Donobedian, Santa Fe, NM.
Page 24: Photo by Robert Reck. Architect: Randall Walton, Albuquerque, NM.
Pages 30–31: Photos by Robert Reck. Architect: Westwork, Glade Sperry and Cindy Terry, Albuquerque, NM.
Pages 32–33: Construction by Jerry West, Santa Fe, NM.

CHAPTER THREE
Page 34: House design by Design Group Architects, Sedona, AZ.
Page 36: House design by Design Group Architects, Sedona, AZ.
Pages 38–39: Photo by Robert Reck. Interior design by Amy Walton, Albuquerque, NM.
Page 40: Floors by Design Group Architects, Sedona, AZ.
Page 49: Photo top right by Robert Reck.
Page 50: Door top right by Design Group Architects, Sedona, AZ.

CHAPTER FOUR
Page 67: Photo by Klaus Kranz.

CHAPTER FIVE
Pages 80: Photo by Robert Reck. Architect: Westwork, Glade Sperry and Cindy Terry, Albuquerque, NM.
Pages 82–83: Architecture and interiors by Design Group Architects, Sedona, AZ.
Page 84–85: Design by Tod Donobedian, Santa Fe, NM.

Pages 88–89: Interiors by Carol Anthony, Santa Fe, NM.
Page 91: Photo upper right by Robert Reck.

CHAPTER SIX
Page 93: Photo by Gene Balzer.
Page 96: Photograph upper left courtesy of Texas Parks and Wildlife, Austin, TX.
Page 97: Photograph by Robert Reck.
Pages 98–109: Renovation by Teresa and Tyler Beard. Interior design by Mark Clay using items from True West Design and the Serape Collection by Ralph Lauren.

CHAPTER SEVEN
Page 111: Photo by Todd Campbell.
Page 113: Bottom photo by Dennis Turville. Photo top right by Linda Mason Hunter.

CHAPTER EIGHT
Pages 130–133: Photos by Robert Reck. Architect: Anthony Anella, Albuquerque, NM.
Pages 134–141: Photos by Robert Reck. Architect: Michael McGuire, Stillwater, MN.
Page 142–153: Construction by Jerry West, Santa Fe, NM.
Page 148: Faux painting and front door design by Melinda Reed and Abigail Ryan, Santa Fe, NM.

CHAPTER NINE
Page 154–155: Photos by Gene Balzer.
Pages 158–163: Photos by Robert Reck. Architect: Bennie Gonzales, Nogales, AZ.
Pages 164–171: Interiors by Georgia Bates, Phoenix, AZ.
Pages 172–177: Interiors by Wiseman & Gale, Scottsdale, AZ.
Pages 178–183: Restoration by Plateau Winds Corporation, Flagstaff, AZ.
Pages 184–185: Contractor: Plateau Winds Corporation (*see above*).
Page 184: Photograph courtesy of *Veranda* magazine.

The use of trade names does not imply an endorsement by the product manufacturer.

www.northlandpub.com

FIRST IMPRESSION
ISBN 0-87358-767-7
Library of Congress Catalog Card Number 00-040189

Hunter, Linda Mason.
    Southwestern style : a home-lover's guide to architecture and design / Linda Hunter.
        p.   cm.
    Includes index.
    ISBN 0-87358-767-7 (alk. paper)
    1. Architecture, Domestic–Southwest, New. 2. Interior decoration–Southwest, New. I. Title.
    NA7224.6 .H86 2000
    728′.0979–dc21   00-040189

80/10M/9-00

To Vanessa "Ann" Holtz, Martina Rossi Kenworthy, and Carol Anthony, for who you are.

KEEP BURNING LIGHT

—LMH

CONTENTS

Vignette from Georgia Bates' house in Phoenix (more in chapter 9). Bench is a Mexican country antique. Small statue is a chair *nicho* saint carried in Mexican parades.

Preface

Why ask a fifth-generation Iowa native to write about Southwestern houses? That was my initial thought when, with apprehension, I signed onto this project. I understand the house part. Not only do I love houses (and consciously anthropomorphize their character), I've been writing about them for twenty years, first for Better Homes and Gardens, then for Rodale Press, later as a freelancer for several national magazines and newspapers.

It's the Southwest part that mystified me. In my career I've walked through countless houses from one coast to the other, explored garden paths, the back corners of musty refrigerators, and anonymous closets of the famous, the infamous, and the little known. Yet the one neglected region in my repertoire of these United States has remained the Southwest—a vast, strange land with uncommon houses and even more unusual people.

When my daughter moved to Arizona twelve years ago I became acquainted with the region, little by little, town by town, season by season. Dedicated to the freedom of the open road, I'd periodically pack up my pickup truck and head out of town toward old Route 66. Destination? The Great Southwest, my house literally on my back, my Great Dane Lucille beside me for comfort and company. As the cornfields metamorphosed into wheat fields, then into a barren landscape of magpies and tumbleweed, I took it all in—the low plains, the wide-open spaces, flat grazing land gradually turning to desert where one-story houses hug the landscape for protection against fierce storms and winds; time-worn New Mexican pueblos, their sun-bleached ladders reaching toward the sun; a scrub desert sea of low-lying piñon and juniper in eastern Arizona where the architecture becomes less Pueblo and more Territorial with each stop telling a whole new story: petrified forest, painted desert,

dinosaur tracks, meteor craters. Nothing prepared me for the moonscape of Gothic sculptured arches and towers amid the breathtaking vermilion canyonlands of southern Utah, where 300 million years of earth's history is written in multicolored, infinitely varied rock layers, and a few eccentric houses are carved into the sides of cliffs, modern-day cavemen taking refuge in the wilderness.

So why ask an Iowa-bred writer to do a book on the Southwest? Because she experiences it all as an alien region, noticing everything for the first time, from blood-red *ristras* hanging on rusty iron porch nails to layers upon layers of geological history to the entrancing smell of homemade bread wafting on smoke trails from backyard *hornos*.

In Santa Fe I met up with Peter Vitale, photographer extra-ordinaire and another ardent admirer of houses. Just as I have spent my career writing about them, Peter has spent his photographing them. We connected instantly. He had an intriguing network and a solid bank of photographs. I had a sketchy outline and a publisher. A collaboration was born. Because money can buy anything, even taste and comfort at home, we decided to spotlight the smaller houses of artists and others with more taste than money in order to illustrate good ideas born of necessity. This is true creativity, we agreed—honest, ingenious, easily adaptable, delightful to the senses. At the same time it illustrates the "quality not quantity" philosophy that's always been at the heart of the Southwest spirit. We tried to give a little history along with inspiring photographs and terrific ideas. We hope you enjoy the result and incorporate some of these thoughts into your own environment, no matter where you live. For that's the beauty of Southwest style these days. It belongs to everyone.

PART ONE Elements

RIGHT: **Weatherbeaten antique doors, painted Taos blue, open onto a courtyard garden creating a** *záguan,* **or walled entrance, remnant of Spanish Colonial architecture.** OPPOSITE: **A rare keyhole-type kiva ruin in Mesa Verde, southern Colorado.**

The Territory

> "The values system that separates us from the natural world is our true enemy—the system that separates the physical from the spiritual. The number one teaching among tribal people is to respect all life."
>
> —DARELLE "DINO" BUTLER, TUNI ("TUTUTNI") AMERICAN INDIAN

THE AMERICAN SOUTHWEST IS A STRANGE, MARVELOUS, FEARSOME LAND. Within the boundaries of five states—Texas, Arizona, New Mexico, Colorado, and Utah—you'll find an incredible landscape of naked desert and jagged mountain peaks, eroded buttes and soft red mesas, sheer ochre cliffs and dramatic canyons, blood-red pinnacles and enigmatic spires, all glittering in clear prismatic light under a brilliantly blue sky—art reduced to its barest essentials. This is the land that time forgot: a haunting place of meditative, quiet beauty framed by sky and time; home to the Anasazi, believed to be America's oldest culture, who maintained a spiritual relationship with the land. For them, nothing was more powerful than earth and sky.

❂ These severe wide-open spaces (long mythologized as a haven for outlaws and loose women) have traditionally welcomed refugees from the dominant culture. Indeed, a certain amount of eccentricity is required for conformity. What they have in common is a rejection of the materialistic ethic in favor of a life lived by instinct.

❂ Here, amid the ruins of time, you learn the lesson of endurance. You come face to face with something so eternal and deep and true it has transformative power. In this surreal landscape you sense a oneness with the world. The very land itself calls for you to respect all life, including your own. "Come on in," the writer Edward Abbey implores. "The earth, like the sun, like the air, belongs to everyone—and to no one."

The Landscape

"Anybody is as their land and air is," wrote Gertrude Stein in 1937. It's true. In order to understand the architecture of the vast area we call the American Southwest, one has to understand the land, for from it comes the forms and materials used in construction. The geometry, dry air, and bright, clear colors of this peculiar, ancient land become translated into the houses of the people who live here, and always have.

This is a colorful land of low desert and high plateaus—an eroded, timeworn topography. On clear, sunshiny days a deep cobalt-blue sky caps every vista, every bend in the road. Abundant iron oxide in the soil colors the earth and rock a deep red. Dimensions of the sky and desert are fantastic to behold. Everything seems intimate, yet far away. Sun and silence are everywhere.

The land ranges from grassy valleys to forested mountains to volcanic mesas to desert so inhospitable ancient people used yucca and creosote bushes for building materials. These ancient people carved and painted curious figures high above the desert floor in canyon walls and beside cave openings—petroglyphs and pictographs—messages from the past saying

who knows what to the modern hiker stumbling upon them. Rich earth yields gold, silver, copper, tin, turquoise, coal, oil, gas, uranium.

The Southwest comprises approximately 900 miles east to west and 600 miles north to south, encompassing all of Arizona and New Mexico, the southeast corner of Utah, the southwest corner of Colorado, and all of west Texas. It's really three locales, each with its own native history and ecosystem: (1) The Colorado Plateau (high desert of mesas, deep gorges, and valleys) comprising the highlands of Arizona and New Mexico from Santa Fe to the Four Corners and, from there, to the Grand Canyon and lower half of Utah, (2) The Sonoran Desert, (an arid area receiving less than eight inches of annual rainfall) consisting mostly of broad, stream-carved valleys and isolated mountains, stretches from the upper Gulf of California into southern Arizona and the western half of Sonora, Mexico, and (3) The Chihuahuan Desert extends from Mexico and includes parts of New Mexico and southwest Texas. Not coincidentally, these were the areas opened to early rail travel in the 1880s, then crossed by improved roads and highways in the 1920s and '30s. Railroads are still important here, transporting goods from coast to coast in snakelike processions up to 120 cars long.

The high Colorado Plateau is a land of dramatic canyons, strange tectonic shapes, and a few volcanic mountain ranges. Forests of piñon, juniper, and ponderosa pine help cleanse the thin dry air. Light here has a cut-glass quality rendering all lines in perfect focus. Lofty mountain peaks twenty miles away appear close at hand. In *An Empire Wilderness*, journalist Robert Kaplan explains the phenomenon: "At 7,000 feet the air loses a quarter of its density, which explains the dreamy combination of sharp, prismlike sunlight and deadly dark shadows—the mark of high-altitude deserts—giving every

ABOVE: High above the city of Santa Fe, photographer Peter Vitale's decktop loggia overlooks the piñon-covered foothills of the Sangre de Cristo Mountains, the southern rampart of the Rockies. On a clear day a Colorado mountain is visible eighty miles in the distance.

OPPOSITE: Rocky desert landscape in eastern Arizona.

image, whether a bare yellow escarpment or a lonely gas station, a one-dimensional, dioramic quality."

In stark contrast, the low desert (a pygmy forest of cactus, mesquite, sagebrush, and scrub juniper) is dangerous and inhospitable—a hard, disobedient land that is neither patient nor kind. Yet it, too, is beautifully magnificent. Here temperatures fluctuate between extremes—sizzling heat at the height of a summer's day to chilly nights under a panoramic sky. Lack of trees leads to a lack of moisture creating notoriously dry air and withering sun. The writer Edward Abbey warns travelers to "Enter at your own risk. Carry water. Avoid the noonday sun. Try to ignore the vultures. Pray frequently."

This varied landscape plays a significant role in housing design. Traditional building materials—clay, sand, straw, wood, stone—come naturally from the earth itself. Smooth, undulating architectural surfaces and unusual geometric shapes mimic features commonly found in the landscape. Construction corners are rounded, with few 90-degree angles. Small windows frame Zen views. Interior decorations spring from the earth, as well—delicate handmade pottery formed from local clay . . . chip-carved chairs and cupboards fashioned from old-growth timber . . . colorful rugs and blankets woven from handspun sheep's wool softly colored with natural dyes . . . tightly woven baskets made of wicker, yucca, sumac, and rabbitbrush . . . curious symbols of etched petroglyphs repeated in stenciled patterns and on light-switch plates. This, in a nutshell, *is* Southwest design.

NATURAL WONDERS OF THE SOUTHWEST

- The Grand Canyon in northern Arizona, carved by the Colorado River over the past 350 million years and containing the oldest exposed rock on earth, stretching 277 miles across northern Arizona, measuring 10 miles wide and 1 mile deep—the most-visited tourist attraction in the world.
- Palo Duro Canyon in west Texas, a 120-mile-long geologic timetable with 250-million-year-old stone at the bottom and two-million-year-old sandstone near the top.
- The Painted Desert of northern Arizona/southern Utah—an eerie, austere, pink desert of eroded red-barred towers, sheer cliffs, and rose-purple sunsets.
- Monument Valley in southeastern Utah and northeast Arizona, a moonscape of buttes and mesas, spires and pinnacles—significant shapes looking like symbols of some long-forgotten mystery.
- Carlsbad Caverns in southern New Mexico, a spectacular honeycomb of caves inside a limestone reef 750 feet beneath the surface of the earth.
- White Sand dunes in southern New Mexico, a sea of white sand stretching for 300 square miles.
- Petrified Forest National Park in northeastern Arizona, containing a spectacular collection of giant fossilized logs and agatized stumps, some complete with root systems, that flourished nearly 222 million years ago.

THE GREAT SOUTHWEST IS HOME TO:

- Fifty American Indian reservations.
- Numerous prehistoric cliff dwellings.
- Phoenix, the fastest-growing metropolitan area in the U.S., a city of dazzling sunshine surrounded by a wreath of desert.
- Santa Fe, the oldest European settlement in the United States, where—at its heart—narrow winding streets look as if they had grown from an Indian trail.
- Los Alamos Scientific Laboratory, where scientists gathered in the early 1940s to assemble the first atomic bomb.
- The Four Corners, the only point in the United States where four states meet.

The History

A pageant of history has left its mark on the American Southwest. Three cultures—Native American, Spanish, and Anglo—came together here, mixing and mingling to create a rich legacy of art, architecture, dress, music, spicy food, and design. Stone Age remains found near Clovis in eastern New Mexico show that human beings first entered the area more than ten thousand years ago. The Cochise people occupied the Southwest six thousand years before Christ.

Santa Fe is even older than Jamestown, the first permanent English colony in North America. The Spanish encountered Indians on Hopi lands almost a century before the English landed at Plymouth Rock. El Paso and its vicinity is considered by some to be the site of the nation's first Thanksgiving.

ABOVE: **Balcony House Pueblo ruin at Mesa Verde National Park.**

THE ANCIENT ONES (TO 1527)

According to American Indian tradition, native people came from another world inside the earth. Research suggests that people believed to be the Anasazi first crossed the Bering Strait during the last ice age thirty to forty thousand years ago. Here, in a span of just fifty-three miles between modern-day Russia and the western coast of Alaska, severe drought lowered ocean waters permitting the first people simply to walk across. At this time glaciers up to one mile thick extended from Alaska as far south as the state of Iowa.

As the massive ice floes melted and receded, dramatically changing the landscape, nomadic hunters travelled further into southern areas following their source of livelihood—large grazing animals—mammoth and bison. Migrations of man and animal continued until the end of the ice age eleven to fifteen thousand years ago.

Ten thousand years ago the Folsom culture appeared, hunting giant bison by surrounding and killing them with spears. Later, the Plano culture evolved. Because the bow and arrow was not yet available, Plano hunters used a variety of projectile points on spears and frequently killed giant bison by driving them over cliffs or into gullies. During 7000 to 6500 B.C. these nomadic people developed the grinding stone, or *metate*. They constructed semi-permanent dwellings, and created basic spiritual beliefs and ceremonies. By 3000 B.C., with most of the big game gone, they began to hunt small game and to hunt in groups.

Agriculture took hold about 500 B.C., and with it the development of culture, social structure, and trading. A second indigenous culture, the Hohokam (Hoho-kám), known for their water-management systems, grew up in the Sonoran Desert around 300 B.C. A third distinct culture, the Mogollon (Muggy-own) people, known for their pottery, settled in the forested mountains of New Mexico and Arizona around 200 B.C. The Hohokam, Mogollon, and Anasazi make up the dominant

EARLY EXPLORATION AND SETTLEMENT (1528–1680)

Spanish friars and missionaries (first Franciscans, then the Jesuits) arrived in the sixteenth century with a twofold mission: to find riches and save souls. They mistook the Indians for pagans and devil-worshippers and set about converting them. In 1528, Alvar Núñez Cabeza de Vaca and other crew members from the ill-fated Pánfilo de Narváez expedition lived among the Karankawa people in southern Texas.

Hearing rumors of seven cities of gold (the legendary Seven Cities of Cibola), Spanish explorer Francisco Vasquez de Coronado led a famous expedition from the city of Compostela, five hundred miles northwest of Mexico City. The expedition traveled north along the Arizona–New Mexico border where they subjugated the Hopi and the Zuni, before continuing northeast across the Texas and Oklahoma panhandles into Kansas. Failing to find any treasures, Coronado withdrew, leaving destruction and far fewer pueblos in his wake.

Equally careless expeditions followed. Utilizing old trade routes, Spanish and Mexican explorers systematically conquered the indigenous people, seizing their farmlands and attacking their religions. In their zeal and haste they destroyed shrines, altars, and representations of old deities, forced the people to accept mission churches in the centers of their villages, and coerced them into adopting Christian beliefs.

By 1598 the Spanish occupied most of Pueblo country in present-day New Mexico. They founded Santa Fe in 1610, and by 1630 had established missions (often elaborate architectural achievements) in nearly every village, using Indian labor for construction. The Pueblo people rose in revolt in 1680, massacring several hundred priests and administrators and sending hundreds more fleeing to El Paso and Mexico. They had had enough.

cultural influences of New Mexico, Arizona, and the Four Corners area. They designed and built fascinating pueblo villages out of mud, grass, and straw, and cultivated domestic arts and crafts—pottery, weaving, basketry. By the thirteenth century, they came together in Taos Pueblo in New Mexico to do their trading, along with several other Indian nations—Kiowa, Comanche, and Apache.

Today's Hopi, Acoma, Ute, Pima, Tohono O'odham, and Zuni Indians descend from the Anasazi, Hohokam, and Mogollon cultures. They still live on their ancient lands, many in houses similar to their ancestors', and many work in the ancient arts using techniques handed down through the generations. They try to live as self-sufficiently as possible, off the land, practicing ancient spiritual beliefs and cultivating the many mysteries of the natural world.

ABOVE: **The ubiquitous pickup truck is the motor vehicle of choice among native Southwesterners, who often drive miles a day to reach the nearest town or village.**

OPPOSITE ABOVE: **Cliff Palace in Mesa Verde, Colorado.** OPPOSITE BELOW: **Tewa girls, Hopi Reservation, Arizona, circa 1906.**

RESETTLEMENT AND EXPANSION (1681–1821)

The revolt of 1680 gave New Mexico's Pueblo people a short twelve years of freedom. Then, on a single day in 1692, without firing a shot or suffering a casualty, the Spanish regained control of Santa Fe and proceeded to resettle the country, this time more quietly and with more respect. By this time the number of pueblo villages was reduced from approximately eighty to around thirty.

During the 1700s Spanish settlements spread throughout the Southwest—into southern Texas, Arizona, and California. At the same time, mountain men brought overland trade in the form of wagon trains, frontier scouts, waltzes, and whiskey. The population grew despite raids from the Navajo, Apache, and Comanche. New Mexico boasted thirty thousand people in 1800, mostly Spanish and Mexicans with dwindling numbers of American Indians. In 1820, two thousand Spanish had settled among the Native Americans in Texas. Spanish friars taught local Indians woodworking techniques, and soon had cheap labor for creating intricate architectural details in newly constructed mission churches.

MEXICAN INDEPENDENCE AND TRADE (1821–1846)

When Mexico gained independence from Spain in 1821, Spain relinquished most of its North American possessions. The Spanish had prohibited trade with the United States, but Mexico encouraged it and a brisk commerce developed. By 1824 the Santa Fe Trail was marked, starting at Franklin, Missouri, and linking the eastern Anglo-American empire with the new western frontier. Merchants flooded the market with tools, utensils, fabrics, and iron nails (a real luxury). In a short span of forty-four years, between 1822 and 1866, thirteen thousand covered wagons transporting $45 million in merchandise travelled the trail, establishing it as one of the United States' main trade routes.

By 1835, after years of conflict with American Indians, Mexicans completely abandoned their Arizona settlements and missions, but American traders, settlers, and explorers had already begun to replace them. That same year, Texas (at the time the northern part of Mexico) sought to become an independent territory. A bloody war ensued. Though Texas lost

1200 The Anasazi move into their famous cliff dwellings at Mesa Verde in southwestern Colorado.

1300 Mesa Verde is abandoned, probably due to prolonged drought.

1539–1542 The Coronado expedition searches for the seven cities of gold.

1680 The Pueblo Revolt drives Spanish from New Mexico territory, but regain control of Santa Fe in 1692.

1000   1200   1300   1400   1500   1600

1000 Anasazi pueblos flourish in the San Juan River Basin.

1493 Cattle arrive in North America.

1598 The entire Southwest becomes part of New Spain. Juan de Onate founds the colony of New Mexico.

1610 Santa Fe is founded. Two years later the oldest public building in the United States, the Palacio Real, is built there.

the Alamo (an old Spanish mission) in a crucial battle near San Antonio, it won the war. For nine years it remained a free republic. Then in 1845 it became the thirtieth state in the United States, causing renewed hostilities with Mexico. When full-scale war broke out the next year, American troops marched off to war following the Santa Fe Trail.

AMERICAN OCCUPATION AND STATEHOOD (1846–1912)

By the middle of the nineteenth century the Southwest still constituted the last extensive tract of unmapped territory in the United States. Mail was carried by hunters, fur trappers, gold seekers, whoever happened to be moving along the trails.

Some thirty Indian nations (each with its own customs and language, many of whom were hostile to each other) remained under Spanish, then Mexican, domination until the end of the Mexican War in 1848, when they came under U.S. jurisdiction. Throughout this time they preserved their traditional cultures as best they could, often maintaining old ways in secret while outwardly appearing to conform to the rules and regulations of the dominant culture.

With the Gadsden Purchase in 1853, the United States acquired from Mexico a great territory that now forms southern New Mexico and Arizona. By 1863, the federal government had divided the territory into four, neat, rectangular shapes on the map representing Arizona, Utah, Colorado, and New Mexico.

In the 1870s railroading stimulated the economy, bringing carloads of ready-made goods to the frontier. The definition of what was "Southwest" followed the tracks. Initially, Missouri, Oklahoma, and central Texas were part of the territory. Later, with the Atchison, Topeka, & Santa Fe Railway, New Mexico and Arizona made the list. By 1880 railroads reached into every section of Texas. The next year the train went as far as Gallup. More than a road, the tracks encouraged social progress and individual initiative, bringing anyone willing to pay the fare to the infamous Wild West.

This was outlaw territory known for its range wars, random shootings, and land-grant skullduggery: the time of Indian wars, broken treaties, and forced relocation of indigenous people to places other than their homelands. At the onset of exploration an estimated one and a half million

1803 The United States purchases the entire Louisiana territory from France, doubling the size of the United States for 4 cents an acre.

1776 The Spanish establish a presidio at Tucson.

1853 The Gadsden Purchase defines today's southern borders of New Mexico and Arizona. More Anglos come to the Southwest.

1845 Texas becomes a state.

1700

1800

1787 Routes of communication are established between Santa Fe and San Antonio.

1821 Mexico declares its independence from Spain. The Santa Fe Trail is marked.

1846 U.S. goes to war with Mexico.

1861 The American Civil War begins.

American Indians inhabited the country. By the late 1800s only 250,000 survived. During those difficult years they saw the loss of their freedom and their way of life. Even today native people of the Southwest are desperately seeking to maintain a hold on their customs, ceremonials, and religions.

By 1900, with the West conquered and the buffalo slaughtered, writers and artists from the East Coast and Europe began flocking to the Southwest, celebrating in their art the rich multicultural mix and ancient artistic traditions they found there. Soon they began arriving *en masse* establishing studios and salons. Health seekers among them put down roots in the salubrious clime of Albuquerque.

A LAND OF REBELS (1913–PRESENT)

The Mexican revolution from 1910 to 1922 brought scores of Mexicans fleeing across the border to make a new home. A series of federal irrigation projects in the early twentieth century accelerated Arizona's development, bringing more people to this western outpost. The 1920s saw a revival in the entire region as newcomers banded with natives to preserve the romance and color of the culture—a rich mixture of earthy Native American, flamboyant Spanish and Mexican, and Anglo rebel influences. Famous artists (including D. H. Lawrence, Georgia O'Keeffe, Willa Cather, Sinclair Lewis, Edna Ferber, Thornton Wilder, Thomas Wolfe, Ansel Adams) set up residence in Santa Fe and Taos, ascribing almost mystical qualities to the light and air.

Route 66, the legendary "Mother Road," was christened in 1926—2,448 miles linking Chicago in the Midwest with the Pacific Ocean at Los Angeles—through three time zones and eight states. Long stretches remained brick covered with asphalt (wooden planks even covered a few short sections) until pavement covered the entire ribbon of highway in 1937. Okies and other Midwesterners fleeing the Great Depression of the 1930s ventured to California and a fresh start along Route 66. On the way they encountered greasy service stations, No-Tell Motels, classic diners dishing up blue-plate specials, hustlers, state cops, wrecker drivers, and anybody else out to make a dime on the caravan of unfortunates searching for a better life.

1858 Gold discovered in the Colorado Rockies.

1869 The first transcontinental railroad is opened.

1900 Artists and writers discover the Southwest and set up communities in Taos and Santa Fe.

1926 Route 66 is christened. Henry Ford lowers the price of motorcars.

1 8 0 0

1 9 0 0

1863 Eight thousand Navajo are forced on the "Long Walk" from northeastern Arizona to a reservation at Fort Sumner, New Mexico.

COLORADO

1876 Colorado becomes the 38th state.

ARIZONA

NEW MEXICO

1912 New Mexico and Arizona become the 47th and 48th states.

By 1954 its heyday was over and a new era had begun. A different kind of refugee became enamored with the Southwestern imagination—Canadians, Austrians, Swiss, French, still more Mexicans, Japanese, Africans—a cool mix of cultures drawn to the colors and the spice. The 1970s saw a boom in major urban centers—Tucson and Albuquerque nearly doubled in size while Phoenix increased fivefold.

Today the exotic strangeness of the Southwest draws all types of people looking for a meaningful vacation or a more stress-free life. On the way they discover the carvings, pottery, blankets, rugs, handmade furniture, healthy diets, and recycled architecture that have come to symbolize the American Southwest.

utah
colorado
Four Corners
Grand Canyon N.P.
Durango
Farmington
Rocky Mountains
Taos
Santa Fe
Flagstaff
Sedona
Albuquerque
Amarillo
arizona
new mexico
Phoenix
Sonoran Desert
Tucson
Las Cruces
Abilene
El Paso
Guadalupe Mountains
texas
mexico
San Antonio

1943 Scientists at Los Alamos Laboratory near Santa Fe begin building the world's first atomic bomb, which is detonated near Alamogordo, New Mexico, two years later.

1930s–1950s Classic cowboy westerns, many featuring John Wayne and Gary Cooper, filmed in southern Colorado and Arizona.

1 9 0 0

1948 American Indians win the right to vote in Arizona.

1957 Santa Fe style codified in Santa Fe, New Mexico.

1984 The last stretch of old route 66 is replaced by Interstate highway.

RIGHT: **Occupied forked-stick hogan, traditional housing of the Navajo. The door always faces east in order to greet the rising sun each morning.**
OPPOSITE: **An old Gothic window sits waiting to be installed in Carol Anthony's strawbale studio.**

The Architecture

"The seasons were linked and formed a circle of life for our people to follow. Everything an American Indian does is in a circle. And that is because the power of the world always works in circles."

—J. REUBEN SILVERBIRD, *THE WORLD IN OUR EYES*

THE SOUTHWEST'S RICH MULTICULTURAL HISTORY IS EVIDENT IN ITS VARIED ARCHITECTURE— amazingly well-preserved cliff dwellings; mathematically precise adobe houses; courtyards of quaint old Spanish haciendas; whitewashed walls of 150-year-old mission churches; inviting *portales* of Territorial ranches supported by hand-carved posts, corbels smoothed with an adz, and the sweat of the homesteaders who built them. Every surface pleases the hand as well as the eye.

⊙ This is a land of do-it-yourselfers. Its history demands it. Rural houses, especially, were frequently owner-built with honest, local materials that spring from the earth: adobe, timbers, stone, clay. Such architecture recalls the rhythms of a simpler life when people took the time to fashion adobe bricks and dry them in sun, carve unique embellishments into beams and lintels, and sit in rockers on the portal listening to coyotes howl. Homegrown Southwestern architecture is richly expressive, often with great artistry and timeless personal style.

⊙ Three easily identifiable influences form the crux of what we call Southwest style:

(1) It starts, of course, with the American Indians, their kivas, pueblos, hogans, and pit houses.

(2) In the 1700s, Spanish settlers modified their hacienda-type colonial architecture to reflect the Indian influence.

(3) With the coming of the Anglos in the early 1800s the architecture changed again to reflect mainstream tastes in vogue in the United States.

The Museum of Fine Art in Santa Fe
exhibits classic Pueblo-style architectural
details—smooth adobe exterior, projecting
vigas, deeply recessed doors and windows
with exposed lintels, even a handmade
kiva ladder at the top.

design style
Pueblo

Next to the kiva, the most important influence on Southwestern architecture is traditional pueblo housing, home to desert-culture American Indians (found principally in New Mexico and northern Arizona). Historically, Pueblo Indians fashioned adobe, stone, and timbers into large, flat-roofed, multi-family houses, which the Spanish called pueblos. Usually built aboveground in a straight line or in a crescent-shape, these one- to four-story mud dwellings were usually two rooms wide with connecting walls several feet thick, but no connecting doorways. For safety, all windows were kept extremely small and there were no doors at the lower level; people simply climbed a ladder to the rooftop opening and dropped into the dwelling. With ladders removed, the pueblo became an effective fort able to resist attack. Several families lived in one pueblo, making them communal structures, some with more than eight hundred rooms.

In pueblo architecture much attention is paid to ceiling construction. Designed to carry great weights, it's a framework of heavy timbers (*vigas*) crossing the shorter span, covered at right angles with a mat of smaller poles—pine, aspen, or willow *latillas*. Packed dirt six to eight inches thick covers the entire flat roof. It was the job of Indian women to maintain outside surfaces by replastering with thin layers of mud, using their hands in nurturing swirls. Thin washes of white earth keep interior walls clean and bright.

Most Pueblo people still live in or maintain a home in a traditional, centuries-old village. Contemporary pueblos essentially maintain the traditional design using a framework of stone masonry instead of adobe walls.

WHAT IS ADOBE?

Making adobe brick is a technique brought to this country by the Spanish who learned it from the Moors, an African desert culture. First, a 2 x 4-inch form is constructed with separate sections, each measuring 10 x 14 x 3 1/2 inches thick. Then, earth mixed with water, using a bit of straw as a binder, is poured into the forms and allowed to dry in the sun. When thoroughly dry, the forms are removed yielding a quantity of adobe bricks, each weighing from twenty-five to forty pounds.

When we think of Southwestern architecture we naturally think adobe, earth mixed with water and straw into a damp claylike consistency.

American Pueblo Indians used puddle adobe, pressing the mixture onto a rock-and-timber framework with their hands, creating a sensuous, undulating texture. Each layer had to dry thoroughly before the next could be applied, a painstakingly slow process.

The Spanish introduced stout adobe brick—adobe poured into forms and dried in the sun—each weighing from twenty-five to forty pounds. Because bricks could be readily produced on site in large quantities, quickly assembled, chinked with local mud, and easily gouged and shaped, this became the primary construction material, especially in New Mexico and southern Arizona in the eighteenth and nineteenth centuries.

Authentic and unassuming with walls sometimes two to four feet thick, adobe makes a solid, reliable structure, warm in winter and cool in summer. By building a double adobe wall—two courses of brick with an airspace in between—insulation and soundproofing are assured. The main drawback: frequent maintenance to prevent the structure from deteriorating. Adobe surfaces are notoriously fragile. To protect the exterior and interior surfaces, coatings such as mud plaster, lime plaster, whitewash, and stucco are used.

Purists believe a mud adobe house forms a spiritual connection with the earth, an organic structure unseparated from the landscape. With its soft lines, irregular walls, and gentle earthen colors, it becomes a kind of fourth-dimensional building material.

Though still in use today, mud adobe is often replaced by cement stucco, which gives a similar rounded, undulating look without the need for constant upkeep. Cement stucco (a mixture of cement, sand, and water applied with a trowel) came into use as an adobe surface coating in the early twentieth century for the revival styles.

design style
Spanish Colonial

When the Spanish settled the Southwest, their architecture combined the most functional aspects of Pueblo and Moorish influences. In cities and towns they built rambling, flat-roofed, one-story adobe haciendas or *plazuelas*. With exterior walls abutting the property line, the entire structure focused inward on one central outdoor area where the well was located. Access to the compound was controlled by a heavy gate and covered entry, or *záguan*, large enough for horses, ox carts, and carriages to enter. These giant doors sometimes contained pedestrian doors, a smaller hinged opening allowing people easier access.

The floor plan consisted of a single line of rooms (each about fifteen feet wide) built in a square or rectangular shape. Each room opened onto the central courtyard or patio and did not have interior doorways or closets. People walked from their rooms into the courtyard in order to get from one room to the other. Usually, each horizontal section was reserved for a specific function: living, service, sleeping, storage.

Covered porches, or portales, stretched along one, two, or three walls, if not all four, on the courtyard side. Windows were small, as protection from Indian attack ruled the design. Roofing consisted of a framework of vigas and latillas, often carved, with latillas laid in a herringbone pattern in important rooms.

Instead of going to all the trouble of hanging a wooden door, settlers simply hung a heavy cloth over interior doorways. Rooms were spacious and interchangeable with high, exposed-beam ceilings and sparse furnishings. Often the walls were mud plaster, the floors made of natural materials: adobe brick, flag-stone, tile, or wide-planked pine.

Smaller rural *ranchos*, on the other hand, stood alone in the mesquite-covered countryside without neighbors and without the luxury of a central courtyard. Spartan and humble by necessity, these thick-walled, one-story frontier houses (built entirely

with local materials: adobe, peeled logs, poles) had all the simplicity of a handmade tool. Uncut stone served as foundation, dirt covered the flat roof (a gridwork of vigas and latillas), the floor the earth itself covered in a mat of furs and skins, or a mixture of mud and water dried to a polish. A parapet often extended above the roof for defense purposes. Mud plaster covered the walls inside and out, sometimes painted with a homemade white-wash or tinted with red mud for color. For ceiling decoration, latillas were often laid in a herringbone pattern, then painted turquoise, red, and green.

Inside, they fashioned all woodwork by hand, constructing small, beehive corner fireplaces with an arched opening and hand-wrought benches (*bancos*) out of adobe. They carved *nichos* (niches) out of walls for storage and display, and recessed *alacenas* (large cupboards) into the thick adobe walls. For decoration they carved geometric designs in corbels and posts, then painted them earthen colors—rusts, yellows, bright sharp blues—using homemade dyes cultivated from the surrounding landscape.

Early Spanish settlers built their own furniture or, if they had the money, hired a local *carpentiro* to build it for them. These pieces were entirely handmade, down to mortise-and-tenon joinery. One of the first items a settler acquired was a large trunk (*caja*) for storing household items. With hardware difficult to come by, cabinetmakers fashioned simple eyelet hinges from bent nails, and hired the local blacksmith to make elaborate escutcheon locks. They often carved intricate motifs into their creations, making them one-of-a-kind pieces. In later years they painted with gesso and natural pigments and added punched tin into cabinet doors.

Exterior architectural details characteristic of the Spanish Colonial period include *canales* (drain spouts); narrow doors and small unglazed windows (for defense purposes); corbels (brackets) for support; and window grills and heavy shutters (as glass was not yet available).

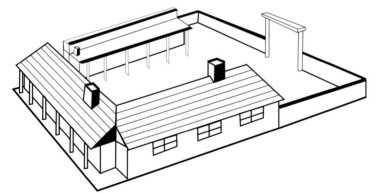

ABOVE: **Some historic Spanish Pueblo-style houses have pointed interior arches, a throwback to Moorish design from old Spain.** FLOOR PLAN: **Hacienda with three separate sections devoted to three separate functions: living, service, and sleeping.** OPPOSITE: **This adobe Spanish Colonial–Style home (located in Santa Fe) has gone through many changes. It was originally built in 1910, but rooms were added in the 1950s and 1990s.**

A classic northern New Mexico Territorial–style house—one-story adobe with steeply pitched tin roof, and full portal with simple Corinthian support posts.

Casa Americana

The first Anglos arrived in the Southwest in the early 1820s, mostly traders and trappers, their belongings strapped into packs carried on the backs of mules. These early frontiersmen built small log cabins as temporary dwellings, much as frontiersmen who settled the East and South before them did.

In the 1830s great wagon trains began to arrive along the Santa Fe Trail. They not only brought homesteaders to the new frontier, they brought a new array of building supplies: tools, lumber, wood pediments, moldings for windows and doors. Construction took place at Army outposts first, where officers and merchants introduced new pieces of furniture—writing desks, daybeds, bookshelves. After 1850 the Army began shipping in large tin containers of food and other supplies. Local Hispanic craftsmen salvaged the containers and began creating their own designs, permitting the old Spanish craft of tin punching to flourish. With the introduction of sawmills and brick plants, more elaborate detailing became possible. Brick coping appeared on the tops of flat-roofed adobe houses.

During the twenty years following the Civil War, Eastern- and European-influenced architectural styles began to replace Spanish Colonial forms. These new houses, built of wood, faced the street and boasted large, glazed windows, high ceilings, and sophisticated neoclassical details like their sisters in the Eastern United States. Throughout the 1880s and '90s more and larger single houses were built with surrounding yards, fences, and garden gates.

The railroad continued to bring trainloads of factory-made building materials—commercial paints, ready-made window sash glazed with paned glass, doors with metal hardware, shingles and metal for roofs, and perhaps best of all—plumbing fixtures.

Each had significance in transforming the architecture. The increased availability of paint spurred its use for decoration.

Windows became larger and more decorative. Window grills disappeared as defense was no longer needed. Options in roofing materials permitted introduction of the gable, dormer, boxed eave, and hip roof—welcome changes in northern regions where heavy snows tended to collapse flat, earthen roofs.

design style
Territorial

In the mid-1800s the Greek Revival style flourished in every state as the architecture of a democratic people. Its crisp lines, soothing symmetry, and neat organization easily adapted to a frontier folk style. Territorial style is characterized by a pitched-roof covered in corrugated tin, a one-story portal spanning the front, and a transom above the front door. Inside the floor plan is arranged around a central hall and entry.

Architecturally, Territorial style blends the best of both worlds—thick, adobe walls lend a wavy, free-flowing appearance while neat neoclassical details (wood trim, pediments, shutters) satisfy the need for order. For renovators, this style offers a variety of interpretations and is great fun to work with. After World War II, wood frame construction finished with brown stucco replaced adobe—a kind of faux adobe—readily available, easy to work with, and carrying a reasonable price tag.

design style
Craftsman

The Arts and Crafts movement gained steady popularity from the 1890s through the 1920s, a reaction against the mass production of the machine age. Philosophically, proponents preached a return to simplicity, function, and uncluttered living for, according to adherents, "Men perish from too much as well as from too little."

The Craftsman idea stressed handicraft—honesty of construction, beauty of finish, simple technique. Soon thousands of Craftsman houses sprang up in neighborhoods across the United States, thanks to a collection of plans published by Gustav Stickley in 1910 and to popular house magazines touting "the ultimate bungalow" designed by two California brothers, Greene and Greene. Common characteristics include a low profile, banks of muntined windows, open flowing floor plan, inglenooks, rustic texture of building materials, broad overhangs with exposed rafters at the eaves, and decorative horizontal banding. Like their Victorian counterparts, these were balloon-framed houses using planed lumber.

design style
Victorian

The train brought a superfluity of machine-age products, changing the look of the house inside and out. Carpenters could now work with milled lumber, scroll and band saws, routers, sophisticated lathes for turning spindles. Due to the availability of milled lumber and the popularity of plan books, carpenters opted for 2 x 4s to frame their houses, and used turned porch columns, cutout gingerbread for roof and porch trim, fancy scrollwork and spindles for decoration, and double porches.

Fanciful Queen Anne styles became the rage, mostly steeply pitched one- and two-story cottage houses with overhanging eaves and gingerbread decorating the exterior. In the mountains, especially, entire towns sprouted a garden of these decorative delights, complete with several gables, a turret or two, and a romantic wraparound porch.

LEFT: **Banks of windows in designer Tod Donobedian's Santa Fe house—each patterned with muntins and different-sized panes—represents a return to handiwork in the Craftsman style.** OPPOSITE: **A tall capped tower, deep overhangs, decorative spindlework and brackets, and prominent roof gable mark this house as Queen Anne Victorian.**

ABOVE: **This pedimented doorway, designed by Doug Atwill, with dentiled cornice and elaborate Corinthian columns, is a good example of a country version of Greek Revival style. The passage leads to an interior garden surrounded by a coyote fence in the center of Santa Fe.** OPPOSITE: **Built in 1927, the Gage Hotel near the Rio Grande River in Marathon, Texas, is a good example of Pueblo Revival architecture Texas-style. A framework of vigas and latillas form the ceilings, turned and carved posts support the roof, and punched tin lights illuminate the portal at night. Guests relax in pigskin *equipale* chairs facing the *placita* (or courtyard) with its central fountain.**

design style
Revival

An architectural revival swept the nation from the beginning of the new century through the 1920s. Just as the East looked to its colonial past for inspiration, so did the Southwest. "Santa Fe Style" (a mixed bag of Pueblo, Spanish, and Territorial styles) has its roots in this period. Spanish-Pueblo and Spanish Colonial Revival architecture flourished, and an eclecticism based on Spanish Colonial, Mission, Territorial, and Pueblo prototypes blossomed. Styles borrowed design features from each other, creating new adaptations: Gingerbread Gothic, Spanish Gothic Revival, Rio Grande Gothic, Pueblo Deco, Mediterranean Pueblo. Bright colors could be seen everywhere as a festive renaissance held the region in its grip. Artists and writers renovating old Spanish houses enjoyed adding their own decorative touches in painting, carving, and molding. Single handedly, they revived the art of decorating corbels and beams. During the Depression of the 1930s the federal government assured a vigorous crafts revival by establishing small schools to teach traditional crafts: furniture and door making, weaving, pottery, embroidery, tanning, tinwork.

town constructed on a high plateau sixty-five miles north of Phoenix in 1970. Arcosanti, which is open to the public, serves as a research and study center for the social, economic, and ecological implications of "arcology," a term coined by Soleri to denote the synthesis of architecture and ecology in a struggle "to develop a culture that might not be so imprisoned by its own needs."

During the 1960s and '70s counter-culture youth found the Southwest climate and landscape ideal for their experiment in self-sufficiency. Though relatively untrained, these rugged do-it-yourselfers revived the building techniques of the Spanish and American Indians, often in creative, noteworthy forms.

design style

Innovative

While the sleek lines and refined elegance of modern architecture swept the rest of the country in the 1940s, '50s, and '60s, most of the Southwest enjoyed a return to a more personally crafted look. Phoenix, the exception, claims several International-style houses, as well as free-form modern houses built in the 1980s and 1990s.

Frank Lloyd Wright, the most famous twentieth-century architect, moved to Scottsdale, Arizona, from his home in Wisconsin in 1927, establishing Taliesin West as his home, studio, and school. Built on six hundred desert acres out of rock, wood, and canvas, the structure wasn't completed until 1957 and serves today as a model for his idea of organic architecture.

Wright's groundbreaking ideas inspired one of his students, Italian-born Paolo Soleri, to build his own model for living, Arcosanti, a prototype for an energy-efficient, socially dynamic

In answer to the environmental and financial woes of the energy crisis, New Mexico became the mecca for passive solar design during the late 1970s and early '80s. Today, innovation continues to flourish as adventurous builders and architects refine the techniques of strawbale and rammed-earth construction in a quest for more energy-efficient, sustainable "green" housing.

design style

Postmodern

Postmodernism was born in the 1950s as a reaction against the cold, sleek lines of International-style buildings. The style peaked in the early 1980s. Basically, Postmodernism turns its back on the modernist obsession with abstraction. It is reactionary and nostalgic, a progressive architecture rich in symbolism and historical allusion, characterized by an almost cartoonish appearance.

ABOVE: **This unusual pair of Postmodern buildings—workshop/studio on the left, family home on the right—could be classified as Neo-Tombstone, recalling old-time western movie sets with their Greek Revival detailing.** OPPOSITE: **Free-flowing organic architecture in the hills outside Carefree, Arizona.**

design style
Santa Fe

In 1957 the city of Santa Fe codified "Santa Fe Style," now strictly enforced by zoning ordinances and including commercial buildings, retail establishments, and housing. Though a self-conscious throwback to both Spanish Colonial and American Indian adobe construction, it is nevertheless an attractive regional architecture suitable for million-dollar houses and megamalls as well as for the poor families for which adobe was originally intended. Key elements include a flat roof, thick walls suggesting adobe, a roof framework of vigas and latillas, earth-colored stucco on the exterior, white plaster on the interior, and a set of architectural details including corbels, bancos, corner fireplaces, and portales.

Another example of Santa Fe Style is the pitched roof adobe-like style designed and built by Betty Stewart during the 1970s and '80s. Rather than flat-roofed Pueblo style, Stewart is credited with revitalizing the tin-roofed Territorial style within the city's limits. Her simple, handsome houses have all the elegance of European-style farmhouses. Characteristics include double adobe walls (two feet thick), comfortably proportioned rooms, high vaulted ceilings, deep portales, and (her trademark) exposed ceiling beams made from milled lumber. She favored traditional raised-hearth fireplaces, brick floors set in sand, mullioned windows, authentic old vigas, antique doors, and fine-textured gauging plaster, which purposely makes the walls wavy.

LEFT: Exposed beams and an elaborate Greek Revival pediment above interior French doors mark this interior as a classic Betty Stewart house, though designed by her brother Pete Stewart and designer Doug Atwill. Spanish and Mexican art accent a white palette—white slipcovered seating paired with English antiques. A wicker chaise gains new life as a coffee table. Skylights added between beams bring in more natural light. OPPOSITE: Antique carved doors in a high adobe wall create an old-fashioned záguan in Santa Fe.

design style
High Tech

In the 1970s the Industrial Aesthetic permeated America's housing. Born of the Industrial Age, it touted surroundings created out of mass-produced materials, reusing prefab industrial artifacts in what it termed "noble" ways—movers' pads used for upholstery, white-enameled factory dome lights in place of elegant chandeliers, steel warehouse shelving instead of teak wall units. Though its strength as a style has waned, it is still an important aesthetic and looks strangely at home amid the soft colors and warm glow of the American Southwest.

Built in 1997, this modern Santa Fe house has international influences as well as Southwestern flavor. Designed by architect Glade Sperry, the 2,500-square-foot house tells the story of its owner, a documentary filmmaker who lost his Los Angeles home in an earthquake. The "story" begins at the entry where a piece of the residence is fractured away from the main body of the house, representing the earthquake. As the journey continues, the "timeline" passes through the Santa Fe environment, represented by a simple geometric rectangular form, which holds the main living areas of the house together. The "timeline" next travels to a circular tower before the final transformation to a new sense of life amid the rugged rock-strewn hills.

RIGHT: **Strawbale construction allows nichos to be sculpted right into the straw. Chicken wire sewn tight to the bales adds strength and holds the plaster or adobe finish.** BELOW: **Workers cover the structure with a mixture of adobe and cement.** BOTTOM: **Courses of straw bales are stacked in a running bond, then pinned with rebar, wood, or bamboo stakes. A chain saw smooths the surface before plastering.** OPPOSITE: **Carol Anthony's Territorial-style strawbale studio outside Santa Fe.**

WORKSHOP

The American Southwest is home to two ancient construction techniques, both enjoying a popular rediscovery: rammed-earth and strawbale building. Both use natural, earthen materials in place of wood balloon framing and both are covered with adobe or stucco to look much like ancient desert architecture.

In rammed-earth construction, forms are built with wood or heavy steel and plywood; then a soil-cement mixture is packed into the forms, eight inches at a time, and tightly tamped down. After the mixture dries the forms are removed, leaving solid earthen walls eight to twenty-four inches thick. The result is an amazingly energy-efficient structure. Since thick rammed earth slows the transfer of heat and cold from the outside, interior temperatures remain stable, making it especially appropriate in arid climates where the temperature swings between extremes from day to night.

The second technique uses bales of straw for construction material, a technique used in the Nebraska Sand Hills where early settlers had no conventional building materials. Modern-day pioneers are choosing strawbale construction for its environmental and energy advantages. Cheap to buy, the bales are easily stacked like huge bricks to make a wall. In a "barn-raising" scenario, it's not unusual for a modest-sized house to be erected in a single day. The advantages are numerous: the walls breathe, bringing fresh air into the living environment; straw bales are soundproof; they are highly insulating, and miraculously fireproof. While an individual stalk of straw will burn, when condensed into bales they actually resist combustion due to lack of oxygen. Before being lathed and plastered, straw bales can be easily contoured into sensuous shapes encouraging dramatic plays of light and shadow.

RIGHT: This new adobe house in Sedona, Arizona, displays classic Southwestern features—carved posts and corbels, even a wooden canale. OPPOSITE: Coverups, like this carved wooden panel, are frequently used in Southwestern architecture to hide utilities or other unsightly but necessary items.

Architectural Details

"When you see a new trail, or a footprint you do not know, follow it to the point of knowing."

—UNCHEEDAH

EACH ARCHITECTURAL STYLE COMES WITH A SPECIFIC SET OF DETAILS. Pueblo style, for example, is characterized by a flat roof and roof beams (vigas) projecting a foot or so out from the exterior adobe wall. Territorial style has a pitched roof and a deep portal with support posts and corbels. But like any regional architecture, Southwestern style resists definition. One architectural design overlaps into another, influences cross pollinate as years go by, making classification difficult. Indeed, cross-pollination of styles and details is inherent in Southwestern architecture, speaking to what the culture is all about.

✪ Though influenced at different times by American Indian, Spanish/Mestizo, and Anglo cultures, one style did not consume or overwhelm the other. Rather, as the architecture evolved, certain motifs, details, and forms became incorporated, causing houses to reflect important aspects of their heritage. Today, this regional architecture is a result of cultural fusion, not domination. It's not typically American, but neither is it Spanish nor American Indian.

✪ Don't be afraid to mix styles. Everything that once had a home in the Southwest's past is welcome in its present. Judicious mixing and matching goes a long way toward perfecting the eclectic look of the Southwest. As long as you use honest materials (the real thing, not some imitation) you'll be halfway home.

RIGHT: Layers of river rock in a variety of shapes and sizes compose this fireplace chimney in Sedona, Arizona. Courtyard floor is local flagstone. OPPOSITE: Talavera ceramics, such as this bathroom sink, are made in Puebla, Mexico.

HONEST, LOCAL MATERIALS

The hallmark of Southwestern construction is its use of natural, local materials in a plan that respects seasonal cycles. Natural materials tie us to the earth, our source of life. That translates to stone hauled from a neighboring hillside, timber felled in a nearby forest, clay dug from under your feet. A structure built of these materials becomes an organic part of the landscape, sometimes almost indistinguishable from it.

This doesn't mean you must use natural, local materials exclusively. Such a requirement conflicts with the nature of building materials in an industrial society. In his architectural bible, *A Pattern Language,* author Christopher Alexander suggests using natural, local materials whenever possible, using them in an ecologically sound manner, and using them to appeal to your senses: touch, hearing, smell, sight.

When building a new house, take a lesson from the American Indian. Be certain the footprint is situated well on its site—to catch prevailing breezes, frame a magnificent view, protect against winter's chill, and provide needed shade in summer.

CERAMIC TILE

When it comes to accents, countertops, shower stalls, and hearths, the lustrous finishes of highly glazed ceramic tile (especially when individually made and hand-fired) are particularly desirable. Made in Mexico, colorful Talavera tiles (an elaborate, interlocking Moorish design that comes in a variety of colors and glazes) are welcome complements in any Southwestern decor.

VIGAS AND LATILLAS

Designed to carry heavy weight, the Pueblo-style ceiling is an intricate framework of large timbers (vigas) and smaller poles (latillas), either pine, aspen, cottonwood, or willow, covering the vigas at right angles. In important rooms latillas may be laid in a herringbone pattern. Sometimes vigas are carved with Spanish or Indian motifs and/or decorated with paint. In more rustic houses, latillas may be replaced with *rajas,* a rough willow with the bark on.

This ceiling in the Gage Hotel is made of weighty vigas covered with latillas laid in a herringbone pattern. Flooring is Mexican quarry tile.

FLOORS & WALLS

Ancient adobe houses had earthen floors, sometimes colored with ox blood and covered with animal skins or coarse home-spun wool carpeting called *jerga*. Brick floors set in sand characterize Santa Fe style. Territorial styles lean toward flagstone or pine plank flooring. We can thank the Mexicans for introducing the warm terra cotta tones of baked Saltillo quarry tile and offering it for sale at a reasonable price. Its orange-red finish makes a beautiful, durable, low-maintenance floor, a fine complement to adobe walls, Indian rugs, and earthen pottery.

Of all these, the most locally indigenous material is mud, used as flooring in desert cultures around the world. Mixed with pulverized animal protein (blood or manure from a cow, horse, or goat) for a binder, mud floors are remarkably durable, absolutely beautiful, and hard, hard, hard. Today, instead of manure, flax seed or linseed oil is used as a binder. Hippies in the Sixties used powdered milk, a government subsidy at the time. Throw a little pigment into the slurry, or mix it with red clay for color.

Floors in adobe Franciscan churches found in American Indian villages are testament to the beauty and durability of mud flooring. After excavation, a course of adobe brick was laid, then covered with multiple layers of thin, mud slurry applied by hand, smoothing in the cracks much like a potter fashions a coil pot. When the right texture was achieved and the mud completely dry, they threw a little grease on the surface, then burnished the surface to a soft glow with a trowel or polishing stone.

Mud cracks as it dries. Some people like the crazed, cracked look, while others prefer a smooth polish. Regardless, a top coat of Damar varnish can effect a finish similar to that of ancient mud floors.

Southwestern adobe walls receive a similar treatment, resulting in either a smooth or a rough surface depending on your preference. Today, cement plaster is frequently used instead of mud. As with mud, pigment can be added during mixing. Mica flakes, too, can be added for a shimmering effect. For a real back-to-nature look, mix bits of straw in the wet plaster.

Luscious paint colors on cement plaster or gypsum board walls create a dramatic backdrop indicative of Southwestern style. Any rich earthen color will do, as long as it fits the color scheme. Try a decorative paint technique—such as mottling, glazing, or ragging off—to create texture as well as color.

ABOVE: **Cement floors in contemporary Southwestern houses can be burnished to look like ancient mud floors found in Anasazi caves. Here, wet concrete was tinted and scored for a decorative effect. Multiple layers of wax lend a leathery patina.**
OPPOSITE: **Mottled saffron wall in Georgia Bates' Phoenix ranch-style house.**

IRONWORK

If you're looking to lend a look of age to a room, installing period ironwork is a wonderful way to do it. Individually crafted ironwork gives Southwestern houses a Spanish colonial accent. When the Spanish ruled the Southwestern frontier, ready-made hardware was hard to come by, so blacksmiths hand-forged and hammered ironwork recycled from weapons or worn tools, especially for hinges and door pulls (though rawhide was also used). Even nails were scarce until the coming of the train in the 1870s and '80s.

Today, though ubiquitous Home Depots and hardware stores make ready-made hardware available just about everywhere, regional blacksmiths still hand-forge beautifully wrought iron-work with its characteristic scrolls and curls. In the Southwest, ironwork is used for gates and signs, branding irons, window and door grills, handrails, fireplace screens, door pulls, bolts, knockers, tools, and one-of-a-kind hinges and escutcheon locks for doors and chests.

METAL ROOF

Roofing in the Southwest takes many forms. Historically, Pueblo Indians used dirt. Navajos use logs in ever-tightening concentric circles in their hogans. Spanish colonial houses sport red clay tile roofs. Some modern-day territorials have concrete shingles, especially in areas prone to forest fires.

In mountain areas where houses have pitched roofs, a metal roof makes good sense. It makes a watertight structure, offers protection against forest fires, reflects the hot sun in summer, and encourages the shedding of ice and snow in winter. Metal roofs have been popular in the Southwest since the late 1800s when the railroad brought tin sheeting to the frontier. Later, corrugated metal became the product of choice. Valued for its strength and durability, it was affordable and required no special tools or skills to lay up.

Today, metal roofing has come into its own as a design element with a variety of colors and ribbed patterns to choose from. Though corrugated is still available, a number of "seam-less" cladding panels exist (each with its own advantages) made from aluminum, painted steel, and a broad range of gauges in galvanized steel. Though it costs somewhat more to install than conventional roofing, a good metal roof should last fifty years or more, thus making up its initial cost. A metal roof can be installed over old shingles without an expensive tear-off.

ABOVE: **Hand-forged iron gate in Sedona, Arizona.** ABOVE RIGHT: **This iron fireplace screen, "Cowboy at the Campfire," is a good example of "tramp art," functional art made during the Great Depression of the 1930s.** OPPOSITE: **Metal roofs on pitched-roof Territorial-style houses are seen throughout northern New Mexico and southern Colorado.**

BUILT-INS

With furniture scarce to come by on the new frontier, Spanish colonists built seating and storage into the structures of their adobe abodes.

Nichos

Nichos, those functional little caves carved into adobe walls, offer opportunity for storage as well as display, and are often used as dramatic backdrops for sacred and highly personal objects. Aesthetically, nichos emphasize the sculptural quality of adobe. They can be vertical (resembling a shell with a rounded top) or horizontal (resembling a shelf). They can be almost any shape, including a Moorish keystone, a stylized Navajo cloud, a variety of arches and ovals, a lyrical conch shell, incised cross, or decorative scallops. Some have a carved wooden base.

Bancos

Bancos, too, are sculptural elements. Spanish settlers built these hand-formed adobe benches along the perimeters of walls for seating several people at once. Because Spanish adobes had one main gathering place, bancos were used to break up large spaces into smaller, functional areas. You often find them built on two sides of a corner fireplace, finished with a *tierra bayita* (light tan) mud plaster, and covered with a colorful blanket. Carried further, some houses have built-in alcove beds—a giant recessed banco—with drawers underneath the beds for built-in sleeping accommodations.

Alacenas

An alacena is a large cupboard recessed into a thick adobe wall. It's usually five or six feet tall and equipped with shelves for organized storage of clothing, dishes, and other household necessities. The doors are always made of wood and can be left elegantly plain or decorated in some manner.

The traditional alacena is simply constructed. Settlers built a wooden frame to fit into a hollowed-out space between the interior and exterior wall. Then they hung a single door with wooden pintle hinges or small hand-wrought eyelet hinges they made themselves, as iron and metal were either unavailable or unaffordable. A few old alacenas contain secret compartments reached by a sliding wood shelf inside the cupboard. Today, renovators are salvaging old wood planks and panels from eighteenth- and nineteenth-century Spanish and Pueblo ruins and reusing them to make doors for these cupboards.

ABOVE: This gaily painted adobe banco in southern Arizona was fashioned over a strawbale framework. ABOVE LEFT: This alacena built into a plaster wall is newly crafted and features drawers underneath, adding to the storage. LEFT: Arched nicho carved into an adobe wall. Pot is by Rick Dillingham.

HANDCRAFTED DETAILS

Individual craftspeople still design, build, and decorate architectural details in the Southwest today. Very few are commercially made.

Lintels

A lintel is the horizontal beam supporting the weight above an opening, as a window or door. It can be hidden behind plaster or stucco, or exposed. In Greek Revival folk houses the lintel is exposed, often taking the form of a pediment. A straight, primitive wooden lintel offers an excellent opportunity for handcrafted detail. It can be carved, chipped, or painted.

Canales

Canales are roof drains or spouts used to carry rain and melting snow off flat roofs to the ground, often onto a splash stone. They were an important functional element in adobe houses and Indian Pueblos as poorly designed or badly located canales could result in rapid deterioration of the fragile walls which were, after all, made of sun-baked earth. Settlers made the earliest examples from split logs hollowed out and lined with galvanized tin. Some are decorated with curved or zigzag designs cut along their edges, incised with simple lines, or hand-carved with rosettes. Most are undecorated, strictly utilitarian objects. Some are supported by corbels.

Corbels

Corbels (a kind of bracket) receive a lot of attention in Southwest design. A single corbel is usually six to eight inches long; double side-to-side corbels measure twice that length. Corbels function to evenly distribute the weight of heavy roof beams and lintels onto a supporting wall or posts. Finely cut corbels are fashioned with saws, then their surfaces decoratively carved or chiseled. Double corbels, carved out of one piece of wood, offer a fine challenge for shape and applied decoration.

Historically, the corbel is the earliest, and often the only, ornamentation found on otherwise plain seventeenth-century Spanish mission churches. Spanish motifs are often carved or painted on for decoration. Popular motifs range from simple geometric carvings to floral designs, gouged bullet carvings, and elegant scrollwork.

Posts

Posts are structural members used to support headers and roofs. Though usually found on portales, they're often found inside the house as well, especially in modern architecture. Posts can be rough or smooth, plain or carved, square or round, elaborately turned or simply formed. In Southwestern design, posts are most definitely handcrafted, and can be tapered or otherwise shaped to suit the desires of the maker.

Portal posts on which corbels rest evolved from plain log supports of the colonial period. These can be decorated using paints; carved using chisels, knives, and saws; or left plain. Popular treatments include a carved rope design, a cruciform design formed by four simple notches, or brightly painted geometrics resembling those found on native blankets and rugs.

ABOVE: Lintel inscribed with the old Italian proverb, "Beautiful mortal things pass. Art does not," a variation of the Latin saying, *Ars longa, vita brevis est* (Art is long, life is short). TOP: Canale on the flat roof of a Pueblo Revival–style house. LEFT: These intricately carved posts and corbels were carved in Mexico and adorn the portal of a large barn on the Blue Lake Ranch in southern Colorado.

WINDOWS

Window styles vary widely, depending on the architecture. Pueblo and Spanish Colonial houses have small, deeply recessed windows that were heavily barred and shuttered. Back then, settlers used doors for light and ventilation, windows for defense and insulation.

Early Territorial houses have ready-made rectangular sashes with small muntined, multipane glass, often with a pediment atop the exterior frame reflecting the Greek Revival style. This can be enhanced with dentils, or left plain. Transoms, too, are typical of this style. Territorial window frames are suitable places for decoration. Grates and spindles keep birds and animals from entering, and people from looking directly into the house. Late Territorial designs have louvered, paneled, or carved shutters added to windows, and curved or triangular designs embellishing window frames. Windows and shutters are often trimmed with jigsaw-cut folk patterns, decorated with applied molding, or painted with various motifs. The pediment is a likely place for a deep incised sunburst or conch shell.

Revival-style houses boast larger windows. By the turn of the century home builders wanted to bring the outside in, so windows grew in size and lost the necessity for grates and grills. Large picture windows can be found in mountain areas where they frame panoramic views.

Window styles in contemporary houses, whether newly built or renovated, should at least nod to the architectural style. But where older houses were dark, today's homeowners covet natural light, so don't be afraid to insert a skylight or two between vigas and ceiling beams.

Look to salvage yards and architectural antique shops for old windows. With work these can become energy efficient and attractive. Select wood, not metal, frames when buying new windows. Metal jars the eye, disrupting the transition from glazing to siding. Historically, rectangular windows are favored over arched and circular ones. Adding flower-filled window boxes helps bring color to the outside wall.

PATTERN TIP   *If somewhere in your house you have a beautiful view to the outdoors, architect Christopher Alexander suggests creating a "Zen view," one of the many "patterns for living" in his remarkable book* A Pattern Language. *Don't spoil the view "by building huge windows that gape incessantly at it. Instead, put the windows that look onto the view at places of transition: along paths, in hallways, in entry ways, on stairs, between rooms. If the view window is correctly placed, people will see a glimpse of the distant view as they come up to the window or pass it: but the view is never visible from the places where people stay."*

ABOVE FAR LEFT: Tall, narrow, multipaned windows with a classic Greek Revival pediment and shutters are typical Territorial style. This Santa Fe Territorial is owned by Jane Smith, a Santa Fe interior designer. ABOVE LEFT: Small, deep windows with interior shutters instead of glazing (like this one in Taos, New Mexico) are typical of old Spanish Colonial houses. BELOW FAR LEFT: In this contemporary house in the hills north of Santa Fe, a large picture window frames a magnificent view of the Sangre de Cristo Mountains. BELOW LEFT: Old Spanish Colonial wood window doubles as shutters for protection against hostile enemies. A lintel was formed above the window in the adobe wall. OPPOSITE: Broad picture windows in contemporary houses (such as this one in architect Michael Mahaffey's house in Santa Fe) are used to encompass panoramic views.

RIGHT: **Designer Ford Ruthling painted a salvaged Mexican door and window cobalt blue, then placed them in an adobe wall as the gateway of his Santa Fe garden.** FAR RIGHT: **This handmade redwood door in Sedona, Arizona, features handmade hardware, as well. The construction is placed in an adobe halo arch.** BELOW: **Salvaged antique and colonial doors and corbels are readily available at La Puerta in Santa Fe (see Sources).** BELOW RIGHT: **Old grilled wood door heralds the entrance to the Powderbox Church in Jerome, Arizona.**

DOORS

Wooden doors first appeared in Spanish mission churches where they were symbols of prestige. Spanish Colonial doors and gates served to keep enemies out and to keep valuable heat inside during winter. Like windows, door styles have changed as architecture has changed. What they have in common is a handmade touch, either in the construction of the door itself or in the decoration.

American Indian pueblos had small roof hatches for doors that were covered with reeds or skins and accessed by ladder. Early Spanish Colonial houses had small doors (two feet wide and four to five feet tall) for defense and insulation. Colonists who could afford to make their own doors adzed large ponderosa pines into hand-hewn panels, using six to eight panels per door. Compact and heavy, they were fastened together by a mortise-and-tenon frame and hung by a simple wooden pintle hinge.

Later Spanish styles favored huge double doors on both houses and gates. Common decorations include diagonal patterns, small panels, flat spindles, chip carving, and patterns made with lead roofing nails (the more nails used, the wealthier the owner).

Territorial doors were often ready-made with milled moldings and pediments set into a plain wooden frame. These are often brightly painted with folk designs or carved cutouts. Sometimes, an awning-type window in the upper part of the door pulls down to expose a screen—a good way for fresh air to circulate in the house without opening the door and admitting flying insects.

Casa Americana doors (built after hand tools, iron nails, and hinges became available) look more like standard batten doors. Gingerbread decorates the plain wood frames of Victorian screen doors with spindles, rosettes, and cutouts.

Folk-style designs evolved from the desire to decorate pre-manufactured doors. Usually, homeowners nailed strips of hand-planed molding or rough-cut lumber onto milled lumber boards, thus creating new and interesting two-ply patterns (sunbursts and crosses are popular). Or, they decorated the door with fanciful jigsaw designs: crosses, stars, diamonds, and other geometrics often painted in contrasting colors.

Pedimented lintels over doors are also decorated with applied moldings. One-of-a-kind screen door frames showcase woodworkers' creativity using braces, spindles, and birds.

Revival period houses often have doors that are carved and painted in individual ways, reflecting Anglo, Indian, and Spanish influences.

Today, even garage doors receive decorative attention. Salvage yards sell antique doors, the ideal accompaniment for true Southwest ambience. Hand-carved doors from Mexico are readily available. For a personal touch, make your own door from old timbers.

FIREPLACES

No Southwestern home is complete without a fireplace. Traditional Spanish colonial haciendas and plazuelas had a fireplace in nearly every room to provide heat in winter. The most popular is the corner adobe fireplace, called a beehive or kiva fireplace, rarely found in other parts of the country. Its design—high arch, shallow shape, raised hearth, reflective interior, fitting snugly into a corner—throws heat out into the room, making it an efficient heater.

A variation of the corner fireplace is the *paredcito*, a fireplace placed on a flat wall with a small, low knee wall jutting out at a right angle, creating an artificial corner. Built-in bancos, kindling boxes, and nichos carved into the dividing wall provide an undulating sculptural element that turns the entire corner into an architectural focal point. When the wall forming the corner is stepped, it is called a *padercita*.

Though often left unadorned, adobe fireplaces are appropriate places for decoration. Common techniques include incising shapes with hatchet and chisel, or stenciling or painting motifs in natural earth colors.

Flat wall fireplaces are also common, particularly in Territorial and Casa Americana style houses built after the Civil War. Some are made of adobe; most are not. Flat wall fireplaces frequently have a wood mantel trimmed with molding. Some even have bancos on each side.

A variation on the fireplace is the *horno* (a conical, outdoor adobe oven used for baking bread), still commonly used in Indian pueblos and in rural villages. According to legend, the horno must be blessed before first use or the bread will come out soggy.

LEFT: **Greg Fitzgerald collects rocks. So, when it came time to spice up the living room of his ho-hum house (built in 1992), he hired a local "rock finder" to help find just the right stone for a new fireplace. These rocks (which weigh a total of 8,000 pounds) come from the Canadian River Gorge in eastern New Mexico. The 6 1/2-foot tall, 19-foot long, 3 1/2-foot deep structure is modeled after a shepherd's fireplace, which was usually plastered and contained a mantel long enough and wide enough for the shepherd to sleep on while staying warm by the fire. The standard flue chimney was first sheet rocked, then sprayed with foam to obtain organic forms, then plastered. A new foundation had to be dug to support the heavy weight.** OPPOSITE TOP: **An old walnut mantel resting atop recycled carved corbels makes a unique fireplace surround. The fireplace itself is in an adobe wall covered with three coats of plaster.** OPPOSITE BOTTOM: **Variation of a Southwestern beehive or kiva fireplace with limestone set into the adobe for decoration.**

RIGHT: **Balance creates order out of chaos in this collection of art and artifacts. A carved, painted Mexican mermaid anchors the design, offset by the tall iron candelabra on the right. Low objects placed in the middle (an old wooden hat, a small doll used in church scenes, a larger Mexican doll used as a mold for doll makers) guide the eye from one end of the composition to the other—a good example of visual flow. Other objects include a wooden Mexican head used in festivals; a classic painted vase by artist Frances Wright, and "The Saint" (a large Fiberglas head by Eugene Jordan).** OPPOSITE: **Egg in architecture by Carol Anthony.**

Soul

"If you can't find where your soul is hidden, for you the world will never be real!"

—FROM *THE KABIR BOOK*

chapter four

SOUTHWEST STYLE INCLUDES A RANGE OF DESIGN CONCEPTS which, when found in combination, conveys a unique spirit of place. More than charm, even more than an intangible feeling of heart, the quality is deep and life-giving. It is, in short, a sense of soul, nourishing and regenerative.
❂ Whether built of adobe, stucco, logs, or plain old 2 x 4s, Southwestern houses manifest this sense of soul in sensual preferences—weather-beaten doors, rough-hewn furnishings, exposed beams, rounded corners, smooth undulating surfaces, earthen colors, gardens and courtyards, one-of-a-kind handiwork, uncluttered living spaces.
❂ Because the Southwest is itself a land of contradictions (both ancient and fresh, commonly visited yet mysterious, predictable yet surprising) design elements are best viewed in contrast—rough hand-hewn timbers against a smooth, undulating wall; prickly yucca baskets next to a pile of woolen Pendleton blankets, a sleek modern Eames chair sitting on a faded Navajo rug.
❂ The current trend fuses this casual multicultural style with the ethnicity of other desert cultures—Moroccan/Turkish, Mexican, even Southeast Asian. The resulting metamorphosis from a regionally based style to a national expression is as comfortably at home in New York, Paris, or Berlin, as it is in Tucson, Durango, and El Paso. It is now truly an international style belonging to everyone.

The Essence of Design

For a house to have that intangible element called "soul," materials, forms, and furnishings need to come from the earth—our source of life. Earth-based materials delight the senses, not desensitize them.

If a home is to manifest soul qualities, some specific concepts need to be addressed. Pay particular attention to natural light, texture and color, surface characteristics, geometric forms, and compositional balance.

NATURAL LIGHT

Clear, prismatic natural light—the kind that draws artists and painters from around the globe—is a mystical feature of only a few special places on earth. That rare delicate light illuminates the high plateaus of the desert Southwest. Santa Fe, especially, is known for its quality of light, thanks to high altitude and no pollution. The light enhances the vibrancy of colors, showing them at their best, whether it's subtle neutrals or bold blues and reds, whether it's on a house facade or glimmering from a cargo-laden pickup truck speeding down the highway.

Light, the life-giving element, needs to be brought into every house. In *A Pattern Language,* architect Christopher Alexander suggests placing windows on two sides of every room to create an interplay of interior daylight with its changing hues and shadows as the sun moves across the sky. He advises paying attention to the color of light, as well. For maximizing the Southwestern ambience, choose room surface colors that (together with the color of the natural light, reflected light, and artificial light) create a warm look leaning toward the yellow-red spectrum.

Window light diffused through a gauze curtain brightens this interior with soft daylight. The rugged wood chandelier, featuring candles instead of electric bulbs, is a replica of Spanish Colonial design.

TEXTURE & SURFACE

Texture lends complexity and scale, detail and depth. Without it, no matter what you do a room is simply not as richly designed. Provide texture in building materials, furnishings, and fabrics. For impact, vary the textures and pair opposites—rough against smooth, hard and soft, coarse with fine.

Texture is best viewed in contrast—smooth hardwood floors next to a large, natural nubby rug, for example, or a plain glass window against a hand-rubbed adobe wall.

Light needs gentle texture to play on, so break up the monotony of large smooth planes (especially walls) by creating texture within them. Old Southwestern houses have the hand-crafted look of adobe or plaster walls. If your walls are drywall, try using one of the new textured paints to create a bumpy sandlike finish, adding much-needed texture. Or, swirl on plaster yourself, creating a touch of the human hand that instantly adds a touch of soul. Rag and sponge painting add much-needed texture, as well.

No matter what you do with texture, it should invite people to touch it. Remember, silk wouldn't sell if it didn't feel so good.

White walls serve as a neutral backdrop for pattern, color, and texture throughout this Pueblo-style home decorated with authentic American Indian artifacts, by textile designer Chris O'Connell.

ABOVE: **Natural "found" objects help create a still life for meditation on the blessings of the earth, its color and contrast.** OPPOSITE: **Four walls—one each of red, purple, green, and gold—are interspersed with a brown and tan palette in this contemporary house in New Mexico. The deep, resonating purple was achieved by first painting the plaster wall with a mixture of universal tints, then adding layers of glaze in light and dark purples with hints of black. Final coat contains streaks of gold to complement the adjacent gold wall. Wall hanging is an 1840s Arapaho Society belt made from buffalo hide and porcupine quill.**

COLOR & CONTRAST

Southwestern interiors mimic the bold, bright colors of the landscape. When it comes to color, timidity won't get you anywhere. For inspiration take clues from the earth itself. Notice the dim blue of far-off mesas; the red, ochre, and soft white cliffs; intense cobalt sky; fiery spring cactus blossoms; bright red chili ristras, strings of blue corn. In this sunny terra cotta place interiors are vibrant, warm, alive.

Use color for decorating window and door frames with brightly stenciled patterns, stylized figures, or colorful floral designs. Paint geometrics or figures on garden gates, porch posts, and window shutters. Or, simply use bold solid colors to highlight interesting architectural features—an arched wooden gate, a particularly intriguing window. Include the region's special colors—terra cotta (a soft red-orange), *tierra amarilla* (a sparkling yellow), Ganado red (the color of bright red clay from a particular area in northeast Arizona). Perhaps the color most popularly associated with the Southwest is Taos blue, a rare and lovely sky blue mixed with a bit of violet believed by the Spanish to ward off evil spirits.

Use these special colors to highlight nichos, windows, or doors. Use pastel washes of color (a mixture of blue and buff, for example) to paint motifs onto walls or to lightly shade walls, furniture, and doors.

To simulate the soft colors of the Southwest in an environmentally benign product, choose natural dyes or natural mineral pigments mixed with water, oil, or wax, then brush, rub, or wipe on wood or plaster.

Available in a range of colors—from butter-cream yellows to rich siennas to vivid blues and earthy greens—mineral pigments can be made into a thick mixture for intense color, or a thin one for a subtle glazed effect.

GEOMETRY

Like the barren landscape with its powerful sky and strange tectonic shapes, Southwestern interiors play on the visual impact of geometric forms. Always done simply and reduced to the barest essentials, this geometry manifests itself in the juxtaposition of closely related objects—the angular openings of windows and doors, or the regular zigzag of an open stairway next to the smooth, rounded surface of an adobe corner fireplace. For impact, these geometric shapes need an uncluttered environment. With the right proportions such geometry becomes almost Zen-like, an object for meditation.

ABOVE: **Geometry in this vignette is pure Southwest, from the Santa Fe home of designer Martin Kuckly. Adobe stepping is part of a turn-of-the-century fireplace surround. Wall is mud and straw. Ram's skull is reminiscent of a Georgia O'Keeffe painting.**

LEFT: **In the home of Erik and Heidi Murkoff, with its minimal furnishings and pure geometry, this foyer (modeled after a chapel) creates an intriguing balance of dark and light, hard and soft, curved and straight, new and old. The ladder, representative of Indian kiva culture, is a fitting sculptural element. The unusual patina of the white plaster walls was achieved with smoke and heat from a fire purposely lit on the floor.**

BALANCE

Balance means visual weight, a kind of visual poetry created by repeating elements to create pattern and focus. It takes into account symmetry, scale, and proportion, as well as flow, so the eye is naturally drawn from one area to the next. You know you've achieved balance when line, shape, weight, texture, rhythm, and color create harmony and variety. The composition should elicit emotion according to placement—either tension, peace, or resolution.

Southwest style plays with balance in groupings, settings, and vignettes, often mixing the three kinds of symmetry (formal, asymmetry, and radial balance) together in a room much as the landscape randomly balances its various elements.

ABOVE: Visual balance is all about weight. In this asymmetrical tabletop composition, the angel sculpture in the center is the focal point with objects falling off to different heights around it. It helps to choose pieces that contrast, such as the delicacy of the flower petals next to the hard stones. Foliage in the bouquet helps soften hard lines. Use small things to fill in awkward spaces. FAR LEFT: Formal symmetry is the balance of mirror images on either side of an imaginary line through the middle of a space. LEFT: In this entry hall, by designer Jane Smith, radial balance occurs when the midpoint of a composition is a dot in the center of an imaginary circle with objects radiating from it at equal distances.

ABOVE: **Adobe walls have rounded corners, giving the structure a soft, hand-finished look.** OPPOSITE: **Sparkling white walls with rounded corners, light pine structural elements, lots of natural light, and a clean brick floor laid in sand set the background for this minimalist interior, showcasing art and artifacts to perfection.**

MINIMALISM

Life is art in the Southwest, so decorate sparingly. Keep the overall scheme simple to help each piece stand out. Minimalism is defined as "the perfection that an artifact achieves when it is no longer possible to improve it by subtraction."

So, edit your treasures. Arrange them amid a few furnishings in a simple, elemental way, but with a sense of true selection. There should be no clutter of what is irrelevant, impersonal, or unchosen. Strive for a look of spontaneity, not calculation. It should look natural and sort of inevitable.

Be careful not to clutter walls, as well. In order to think clearly, the artist Georgia O'Keeffe preferred empty walls. She believed the more you had on the walls, the less chance something new would enter your mind.

ROUNDED SURFACES

The very nature of adobe lends itself to round, undulating surfaces inside and out. Its sculptural quality creates walls that flow organically into bancos and nichos, projections and recesses that function as furniture while giving a sense of openness to the room. Because, from the beginning, adobe was the building material of choice in much of the region, rounded corners and undulating surfaces have become symbolic of Southwest construction. It shows the caring touch of the human hand and all that imparts and symbolizes, opposed to straight, square lines—a sure sign of machine-built construction materials.

The exquisite handmade look of adobe can be achieved in houses built with modern 2 x 4s and drywall. Carpenters make rounded corners using flexible metal strips at drywall corners. The swirls of a human hand on undulating wall surfaces can be achieved using plaster or one of the new lightweight stucco-like materials, such as Dryvit, which can be shaped to fit any form and can be used on both interior and exterior surfaces.

Objects and Accents

Of the many delights of the desert Southwest, its handicrafts stand alone as testament to the endurance of the creative spirit. American Indian carvings, canvases, pottery, blankets, baskets, rugs, sculpture, rawhide drums, and jewelry have come to symbolize the rich ethnicity of the region.

Contemporary American Indian art takes an abstract form, an exciting evolution of ancient traditions. Southwest style blends these handicrafts with Spanish and Mestizo influences—chip-carved chests and furniture, elaborate punched tinwork, colorfully painted pottery, primitive country antiques, applied moldings and fancywork on chests and tables—as well as with handmade objects from family and friends.

TINWORK

A purely Spanish folk art, decorative tinwork has a rich tradition on the Southwest frontier. Historically, tinsmiths fashioned religious objects from tin, usually storage containers discarded by the American Army. Today, they hand punch, stamp, and emboss tin into several marketable household items—wall sconces, lamp shades, switch plates, nichos, mirror frames, chandeliers, even furniture. Because punched tin reflects light, its use in light fixtures creates intriguing shadows with its enlarged pattern on walls and ceilings. Punched tin is also found in doors to pie safes and cabinets where it allows air to circulate inside the cabinet while keeping out flying insects. Some artists enhance the patina of tinwork by exposing it to the sun, thus obtaining the appearance of deep red leather, well-worn copper, or verde brass.

ABOVE: **Various tin rosaries and *milagros* dating from the early 1900s decorate the hide shade of a rustic pottery lamp.**
RIGHT: **A contemporary take-off on a traditional tin retablo.**

POTTERY

What makes Southwestern interiors so special is the mixture of Indian pots and blankets with Spanish rugs and furniture. Pottery plays an important role here, as each Native American tribe has its own style. Whether Hopi, Navajo, Pueblo, Acoma, or Zuni, whether old or new, traditional or modern, Indian pots with their earthen colors, bold geometrics, and primitive figures definitely have a place as accents in Southwestern interiors. Mexican pottery, with its bold colors and brightly glazed paint, has a place, too. Just be careful not to eat food from a bowl, plate, or platter painted with toxic lead-based paint.

TEXTILES

Hispanic and American Indian embroidery and weaving fit naturally in any Southwest-style home. It was the Spanish, in fact, who brought sheep to the region, thus starting a whole new industry. Southwest Indians wove beautiful blankets on looms and used them as wraps, much as we use coats. In the late 1800s Anglo traders convinced them they would make money for their weavings if they made rugs instead of blankets—thus the beginning of a new tradition.

Textiles come in a variety of patterns, from bright, simple geometrics to stripes, lozenges, and leaves. Rio Grande blankets (typical of everyday textiles used in Spanish colonial homes in the nineteenth century) and Pendleton blankets make colorful accents. In fact, legend has it that in the 1920s and '30s Navajo rug makers preferred washable Pendleton blankets and would often trade one of their own handmade rugs for a colorful Pendleton.

ABOVE: **This collection of original Pueblo pottery (Santo Domingo, Acoma, and Zia) dating from the 1920s represents a spiritual journey for its owner, fashion designer Michael Robinson, who appreciates the simplicity of its origins and the beauty of the craft. Robinson collects each piece individually.**

RIGHT: **Rio Grande and Saltillo blankets, piled high upon a worn Spanish Colonial chest, lend texture in their silk and wool weave with dangling silk fringe, in Chris O'Connell's home.**

RIGHT: In antique dealer Fred Pottinger's home, rare and hard-to-find *bultos* (wooden figures of Catholic saints) are hand-carved, brightly painted, one-of-a-kind objects highly collectible in the Southwest today. OPPOSITE: Kachina dolls (in the Hopi tradition) are meant as teaching aids, not playthings. In religious dances and ceremonies, real live kachinas (Indians in costume) bring the spirit world to life in a festival of magic and learning. A Wuyaqtaywa (Broad Face) kachina by Hopi artist, Tay Polequaptewa.

The Magical and the Sacred

The cultures that initially settled the Southwest viewed the Great Mystery from entirely different perspectives. For the Native American, harmony of soul was most important. One achieves such a delicate balance with respect for all living things. "To respect the Earth and each other, to respect life itself. That's our first Commandment, the first line of our Gospel," teaches Mathew King, Lakota wisdomkeeper.

For the American Indian life is an artful poem replete with symbolism and metaphor. It is a maternalistic culture, revering the fertility of the earth as our mother. Her race sprang from inside the earth into this world of material beauty. All myths and legends grow from this rugged environment—its whimsy, its lessons, and its wonders. Temples and shrines exist solely in nature. She burns sweet grass and sage to purify the air, and often builds her house in a circle, the most sacred shape, for it is never-ending. She honors the four seasons and prays every morning to the four directions. Water is her lifeblood. Because she depends upon the fruit of the earth for survival, she develops an ecological philosophy of earth nurture. She believes in spirit guides and prayer feathers, and strives to live with a constant sense of peace and beauty, in harmony with all that surrounds her.

Spanish Catholic priests and missionaries, devout though they were, mistook this earth religion as paganism and saw the Indians as devil-worshippers and heathens. In contrast to the maternalistic society of the Indian, their Catholicism was a paternalistic, hierarchical society clothed in human iconography. Instead of honoring the earth, they believed in two supreme male spirit figures—God the Father and God the Son. Eternal life was assured through good works.

In the seventeenth and eighteenth centuries, Franciscan and Jesuit friars established missions in nearly every Southwest village and built sparkling white adobe churches, filling them with symbolic imagery in the belief that that alone would illuminate the path to the divine. They believed dead saints could hear whispered prayers before their icons and would thus grant the wishes of the devout. Carved wooden figures of very human saints (*bultos*), flat-painted *retablos* depicting Biblical stories, simply rendered altar screens (*reredos*)—this is great folk art, and highly collectible.

When Mestizos from south-of-the-border began populating the Southwest in the early 1900s, they brought colorful pageants and fiestas with them, introducing a magical spirit world beyond the realm of everyday reality. They depicted inhabitants of this netherworld in hand-carved wooden masks—demons, animals, insects, reptiles, birds, humans, skeletons. These masks, according to tradition, capture the spirit of the maker as well as the spirit of the wearer and the spirit of the figure depicted. They warn about the folly of wearing one casually, for spirits are alive in it. This, coupled with a theatrical Catholicism based upon the legend of the Virgin of Guadalupe, and in images of agonized Christs and dolorous Virgins, sums up the Mexican input into Southwestern religious iconography.

All these magical and sacred objects—from simple stones to gaudily decorated altars—are part of the high color that is in the landscape and the gardens and all of it finds a place in the Southwest-styled home.

Spanish and Indian Motifs

Both American Indians and Spanish colonists painted, carved, and otherwise decorated their houses with motifs stemming from their culture and their beliefs. Typical Spanish decorations include rosettes, half shells, pomegranates, crosses, stars, and diamonds. Indian patterns come from nature—stylized birds, harvest and corn motifs, clouds and lightning, flowers, feathers, animals, and the spirits they represent. They, too, decorated with stars, diamonds, and other bold geometrics.

These symbols find their way into both the architecture and the interior design of today's Southwest houses. Such symbols can crop up anywhere, even in a radiator cover, shower wall, or garden sculpture. Let your imagination be your guide.

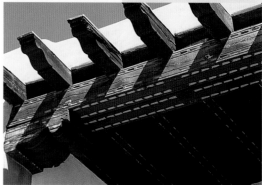

LEFT: A series of washes covered with wax helps give the walls in this Spanish Colonial home a rich, aged look. The *trompe l'oeil* paintings around the doorways were modeled after old carved Mexican window casings. Artist Cynthea Peck incorporated grape clusters and the homeowners' initials to personalize the Spanish-inspired graphic in this wine room. Carved door (purchased from La Puerta in Santa Fe) is from India. OPPOSITE ABOVE: A stylized Navajo lightning pattern cut into this custom-built radiator cover in Flagstaff, Arizona, allows heat to infiltrate indoor air without the necessity of seeing the radiator itself. An Acoma pot, decorated with characteristic scrolls and symbols, sits atop the cabinet. OPPOSITE BELOW: A series of painted bullet carvings on beams and corbels in a Santa Fe public building are reminiscent of the Spanish Colonial tradition.

RIGHT: Where else would you find such grand shabby elegance, but Texas? This industrial building in San Antonio is filled with old-world furnishings. The owner, interior designer Gwynn Griffith, travels the world in search of treasures. Glazing on the walls achieved an old-world patina. Plaster ceilings are left exposed and painted an Italian blue; exposed brick frames new steel windows. Italian marble surrounds the fireplace. Original wood floors are oiled and covered with a Turkish rug. The chandelier is one of a pair of Venetian lanterns dating from the seventeenth century. German chenille covers the sofa; mohair plush velvet covers the reproduction Louis XVI chaise, while tiger-stripe silk velvet graces the ottoman. The nineteenth-century painting is reminiscent of Spanish *retablos,* but on a larger scale. OPPOSITE: Everything in Carol Anthony's Santa Fe kitchen is made of natural materials, "except the ice cube trays," which are plastic.

Rooms

chapter five

"With beauty before me, I walk.

With beauty behind me, I walk.

With beauty above me, I walk.

With beauty below me, I walk.

With beauty all around me, I walk.

In beauty, it is finished."

—TRADITIONAL NAVAJO PRAYER

LIKE THE ARCHITECTURE ITSELF, ROOMS IN SOUTHWESTERN HOUSES HAVE EVOLVED OVER TIME. Though surfaces are much the same (natural materials, natural hues), furnishings have changed with the passage of time. American Indians furnished sparsely and primitively. Spanish colonists furnished sparsely and pragmatically. Anglos furnish for comfort and efficiency.

❂ Today's eclectic look emphasizes personal style. As long as a room contains a few traditional architectural elements (banco, corbel, arch, or hand-hewn beams, for example) you can furnish it judiciously however you choose and still achieve a Southwest look.

❂ Surprisingly, though history has altered the way rooms look, how rooms are used has not changed much over the past five hundred years. The living room, with its raised hearth, is still the central gathering place for family and friends. Generous hospitality shines in the dining room or eat-in kitchen, wherever the table is large enough to hold a sumptuous spread. The main bedroom is the quietest spot, a large retreat furnished in restful hues.

❂ The room most drastically altered over time (besides the bathroom, which was a privy out back until the turn of the century) is the kitchen, where the introduction of modern appliances and the need for consummate efficiency preempt any desire for historical accuracy.

When clothing designer Michael Robinson moved to a new, contemporary Pueblo-style house in the Santa Fe hills, he chose a light palette for the background (timbers of ponderosa pine, smooth walls with rounded corners). The architecture gives a nod to Spanish Colonial style—vigas, exposed lintels, brick flooring set in sand (in a herringbone mosaic pattern), a corner fireplace with padercita. White cotton slipcovers on chunky chairs and sofa both look good to the eye and feel good to the touch. A *kilim* rug covers an ottoman. Michael found the scrolled iron mantelpiece (rumored to have hung above a doorway in an Argentinean church) at a flea market. He was drawn to the item because it looks so delicate, yet is extremely heavy.

Gathering

The Southwestern gathering room is always a casual, informal spot—nothing snooty or overly polite about it. Before Spanish colonization, American Indians gathered around a campfire or in the kiva (an underground room used for meetings and worship reached by a ladder from the top). The haciendas of important Spanish colonists had a large central *sala* with a raised hearth and bancos ringing the perimeter for seating lots of guests at dances and fiestas. Anglos made this a "living" room for the gathering together of family, friends, and neighbors.

Today, the gathering room is used more for conversation than for dancing. The secret to creating a room conducive to good conversation is to group chairs, sofas, and benches in a welcoming sitting circle, advises architect Christopher Alexander in *A Pattern Language*. Arrange seating loosely, to suggest a circle but not demand it. A few too many chairs make a welcoming invitation. If your room is large, create several small conversation areas with furniture groupings.

Hospitality

Communal eating plays a vital role in most societies, and has since humans first broke bread together. Sharing food and sustenance binds people together in a universal way. Gracious hospitality has been an important part of Southwestern life throughout its five-hundred-year history. Partly because the desert itself is so remote and inhospitable, cheerfully treating guests and travelers to food, drink, and sometimes lodging becomes a moral responsibility. Ceremonials and festivals draw guests from far away for many days at a time, making hospitality a cornerstone of the culture.

Not much has changed, really, from the old days. Willa Cather's 1930s novel *Death Comes for the Archbishop* describes a frontier New Year's party in the mid-1800s: "The house was full of light and music, the air warm with that simple hospitality of the frontier, where people dwell in exile, far from their kindred, where they lead rough lives and seldom meet together for pleasure."

In the Southwest today the eating table enjoys a central location large enough to serve whole groups of people for celebrations—wedding feasts, birthday parties, Christmas dinners, wakes, evening meals. Since frontier life is casual, it doesn't matter if the table is located in the kitchen or in the dining room—whatever suits the way you live works best.

PATTERN TIP *In* A Pattern Language, *architect Christopher Alexander advises having a light over the table to create intimacy, bringing people together in its soft glow, rather than maintaining the same light level over table and walls. A low, soft light over the table lights up people's faces, especially when background walls are dark.*

Table and chairs come front and center in the dining room of Michael Robinson's contemporary adobe house. The pegged, wood harvest table is an Italian antique. Costes side chairs (designed in 1982 by Philippe Starck for the Cafe Costes is Paris) have tubular steel frames, three legs, and plywood backs. Mexican santos surround the table, appearing to float on plexiglass pedestals, especially in candlelight.

The Kitchen

Southwestern kitchens work best as big, bright, welcoming rooms with enough space to comfortably hold a large table and chairs. Typical Southwest design has counters ringing the perimeter, along with stove, sink, and refrigerator. Ceramic or quarry tile surfaces usually make an appearance. Wood planks cover the floor.

Before 1900, a large, open fireplace was used for cooking in the kitchen, along with a backyard horno for baking bread. Caves dug into the ground kept foods cool. Many foods were dried, as the arid sunny climate provided the perfect environment and local cuisine (frijoles, red and green chiles, blue corn, apples) gained intense flavor and longer life when dried. Today, we have a myriad of handy appliances to make kitchen life easier.

Choose hard-working appliances—a large, energy-efficient refrigerator, a deep sink with gooseneck faucet for filling buckets and soup pots. Select your range (a symbol of nurture) with care and make it a focal point. A commercial range (with more room between the burners for large pots and skillets) works well for gourmets and large families. History buffs go for picturesque old enamel stoves (some with a warming oven) restored to work in modern kitchens. Whatever you choose, make sure it fits your needs before you lay out the cash.

Though located in an old adobe house, this organic contemporary kitchen does not feel out of place. The clean, simple look mixes earthy materials—granite countertops, slate tiles for backsplash and floor, brushed steel cabinets. Eames chairs and matching tabletop offer a pool of golden light in the otherwise monochromatic scheme. The tabletop matches the chairs while the table's legs match the cabinets.

Built in 1845, art dealer Jim Kelly's Santa Fe house juxtaposes worn hand-hewn historic features (smooth hand-plastered adobe walls, rough-cut vigas) with hard-edged modern furnishings, set against a minimalist white backdrop. The bed is raw steel with a gray patina. Chairs are Le Corbusier. Shelving is steel and glass. Floor is brick covered with a short-nap wool rug. Black-and-white movie stills complete the scene.

Sleeping

Before the nineteenth century, bedrooms were a luxury. People slept on the floor upon cotton mats stuffed with straw or wool, using animal furs for bedding. They didn't start sleeping off the ground until the mid-1800s when the Santa Fe Trail opened an avenue for American commerce, bringing spindle and daybeds to the frontier from the East.

Today, sleeping occurs in private rooms. The largest is the couple's realm, a quiet spot off-limits to children. In the Southwest it's as restful and serene as possible with peaceful colors and little clutter. For the children, consider a cluster of beds amid a large play space. This keeps young children from feeling isolated in a room of their own.

Southwest houses usually have guest quarters to accommodate visiting friends, relatives, and wandering iconoclasts. These take the form of a separate guest house, a private room, or corners carved out of public spaces (a curtained alcove in the gathering room, a daybed on the portal).

PATTERN TIP

In A Pattern Language, *author Christopher Alexander advises considering the importance of the marriage bed, for it is the center of a couple's life together. It's "the place where they lie together, talk, make love, sleep, sleep late, take care of each other during illness." He suggests finding a way of adding to the bed and the space around it over the years, so it becomes more personal and unique as time goes by. Purchase a headboard that can be carved, painted, or repainted, he suggests, or create a bed enclosure that can be changed, maybe embroidered.*

Bathing

Before the advent of indoor plumbing, people used the court-yard fountain to bathe, or a nearby river, or a tub filled with sun-warmed water. Around 1900 the bathroom moved inside the house. Today, it's more than a sterile compartment for the toilet. It's a complete bathing facility—often with two sinks, a shower, and a soaking tub—that makes the act of ablutions both therapeutic and pleasurable.

A Southwest-style bathroom has tiled surfaces—a good place to showcase colorful Talavera tiles and ceramic sinks. Be careful with tile floors, though; slippery surfaces make for nasty falls. Keep safety in mind, both when designing the bath and when using it. More accidents happen here than in any other room of the house.

Make sure the room has plenty of light. Provide access to a walled garden, if possible. Consider adding a skylight over the shower or tub. For added privacy, house the toilet in its own walled compartment.

LEFT: **In antique dealer Gloria List's bathroom, a warm bubble bath in a giant clawfoot tub (from Kohler) awaits someone special, a chapel of sorts amid gleaming candles and Spanish colonial accessories.**
OPPOSITE: **This contemporary Industrial-style bathroom features a steel pedestal sink textured with a firm wire brush. Basin and fixtures are from Kohler. Raw plaster walls and stained concrete floor complement each other, creating a monastic feeling. (The rest of this house is featured on pages 30 and 31.)**

Guest Quarters

Welcoming travelers is a Southwestern custom. Because towns are spaced miles apart and the desert is so inhospitable, putting up travellers for the night was a historical necessity. Hacienda-type floor plans often incorporate guest quarters complete with private bath, fireplace, and direct access to the central court-yard. Other plans incorporate a small guest house (perhaps only 300-square-feet) somewhere on the grounds, or over the garage. If none of these options work, a guest room in the main house can be reserved for frequent visitors.

Steve and Connie Segnor's new Sedona, Arizona, adobe house has guest quarters at one end of the hacienda-style floor plan. Its only door opens onto the court-yard. Like the rest of the house, the guest room is furnished in Craftsman style with a waxed, scored, and colored concrete floor in a geometric pattern. There's a small entry hall, bedroom with beehive kiva fireplace, and a small bathroom with a clawfoot tub.

The Portal

More than any other architectural element, even more than the corner kiva fireplace, the portal is the Southwest's number-one contribution to American architecture. It's found throughout the Southwest, from southern Colorado and the range lands of Utah to west Texas, northern New Mexico, and the sagebrush plain of Arizona. The long, deep covered porch spans the facade on ground level so you walk directly from the portal into the courtyard or street. It shields the house from direct sun, and can be found on either front, rear, or both facades, whichever faces south or west, thereby receiving the most intense heat. Back walls are frequently painted white to reflect light deep into the space. The roof is a wood framework supported by posts, sometimes capped with corbels.

Like the pitched roof in rural houses, the portal is often an added element. When found, its personality is an important clue to the character of the house, a fitting place for decoration. Carvings and/or paintings delicately embellishing architectural details (posts, lintels, corbels, beams) put a personal stamp on the architecture itself. When old and in good shape, these decorated pieces make valuable antiques.

Furniture in the portal is weather-resistant, practical, and comfortable. A fireplace, even a daybed, can be found here. South-facing portales are ideally sited for renovation into sun rooms.

Some portales make excellent candidates for conversion into sunrooms. This one, remodeled by designer Tod Donobedian in Santa Fe, has radiant-heat flooring, making it delightful in all seasons. Before renovation, the wall with the triangular relief sculpture was the exterior wall.

Patios and Courtyards

The great outdoors has always played a key role in Southwestern living. Warm days, cool nights, and an arid climate discourage pesky insects, making an ideal environment for life *al fresco* at least nine months out of the year.

Before Spanish colonization, Southwestern Indians congregated in central village plazas under the bright blue sky to do their trading. The Spanish purposely built their haciendas around an enclosed courtyard, or placita, for protection against enemies as well as for privacy and enjoying the weather. Anglo settlers cultivated outdoor areas for gardens, informal socializing, and dining al fresco.

The Southwestern patio or courtyard is usually paved with stone, brick, or tile, and sometimes contains a central well or fountain. Enclosures of low walls and shrubs give the feeling of an outdoor room under open sky. Sometimes there's a fireplace, bancos, nichos, and a perennial garden of native flowers and plants (sun-loving varieties—poppies, hollyhocks, daisies, and buffalo grass with potted geraniums as accents). If a vegetable garden exists, a simple irrigation system running through the garden may be a necessity. Whether you want a private shade garden or a great multi-functional area for cooking and entertaining, a patio and/or courtyard expands the repertoire of rooms and celebrates the simple pleasures of the out-of-doors.

ABOVE: **With a breathtaking view of the Sangre de Cristo Mountains, this flower-filled 35 x 50–foot courtyard is as frequently used as any indoor room. Flagstone flooring complements the adobe walls. Since snow rarely overstays its welcome in Santa Fe, the mantel and shutters remain outdoors year-round while the furnishings retire for the winter.**
OPPOSITE: **This central courtyard fountain in old Santa Fe is typical Spanish Colonial design, surrounded by a garden of flowers blooming amid the sunshine and blue skies of a typical New Mexico summer's day.**

Sacred Spaces

Southwestern houses historically contained an altar of some kind, a visual symbol of spirituality if not religion. For American Indians that altar was anywhere outdoors, for they worshipped nature. Spanish colonial haciendas often contained an oratorio, or chapel, brimming with bultos, retablos, and burning votives to facilitate prayer. Anglo artists in the 1920s expressed their spiritual beliefs through carvings and paintings in the structure of the house itself. The artist Georgia O'Keeffe composed tiny shrines of natural, found objects—stones, feathers, shells—in meditation nichos throughout her Taos adobe dwelling.

Today the yen is for a yoga room, a meditation corner, or a quiet room of one's own—a silent, reverent space belonging to one person alone. A place to stop the clock, go inside, find your center. A place of personal nurture, contemplation, renewal. The key to such a room is to make it comfortable and tranquil, so you want to be there. Decorate with personal objects—old postcards and photographs, wildflowers, found rocks, mementos; bits gathered from walks.

Artist Carol Anthony has several sacred spaces on her five-acre Santa Fe compound, but the one closest to her heart is a chapel off the bedroom garden—a quiet, peaceful place dedicated to the memory of her twin sister, where Carol goes to be alone with her feelings and her thoughts.

Made of straw bales, the chapel in artist Carol Anthony's Santa Fe cloister is 8 x 10 feet and attached to the house, though the only door is located off the bedroom garden. Here, the soft sounds of classical guitar weave through the air, a mesquite fire smolders in the kiva fireplace, and a candle remains lit, day and night, in memory of her twin sister, Elaine, also an artist, who recently died of cancer. Carol has peopled this room with lots of old pictures—twins, the beach, Elaine's hands—as well as an old child's gown in a frame (Carol's house is featured on pages 142–153).

Furnishings

Antique furniture, especially primitives, add honesty to any Southwestern decor. Because the region is so ethnically varied, it doesn't matter where the antiques come from, as long as they're well made, functional, and suit you aesthetically. European influences have always mixed well with Mexican in the Southwest—gilded mirrors or an English highboy set against a handmade Navajo rug, for example. Together they say beauty exists among all people. African or Asian influences mix well, too.

For historical authenticity, nothing beats rugged Spanish colonial antiques, for no matter where you go in the Southwest the Spanish preceded you there. Material comforts were few on the Spanish frontier of the 1700s. Only wealthy families and dignitaries could afford common luxuries such as furniture. When they could, Spanish settlers hired carpentiros to fashion a sturdy piece or two to suit their needs—chests, tall cabinets, footstools, plain chairs—charming folk-art furnishings made with simple tools and simple techniques. These handmade pieces tend to be massive and crude, for they were made from forest timbers felled with an axe or a two-handed bucksaw, then adzed to a smooth plane rather than sanded. Early carpentiros used mortise-and-tenon joinery to construct their furniture, tediously making both mortise and tenon by hand using a sharp knife. By the nineteenth century, dovetail joints and tongue-and-groove edges became commonplace.

Today, the most coveted collectibles are handmade wooden benches decorated with carvings (made to serve as a family's church pew as well as for seating in the home); the *caja*, or chest, made by joining four side boards together with a dovetail joint, then attaching the top and bottom by pegging or metal hinges; the *trastero*, a tall upright cupboard, often a showcase of the carpentiro's skill and a favorite of modern collectors, and the *harinero*, a rare though much sought-after grain chest often accompanied by sifters and stone metates used in the preparation of grains.

When authentic antiques cannot be found for a reasonable price, Mexican primitives offer a viable substitute. Several regional shops supply customers with a reliable conduit to Mexican artisans. One, El Paso Import Co., deals exclusively with primitives from the Mexican countryside and small villages, and has shops throughout the western United States (see Sources).

Southwestern antiques mix well with other country antiques. In fact, the mistake people often make is not mixing enough. The whole point of personal design is an eclectic mix, not just one style. The secret is to keep the overall scheme simple so each piece stands out. Interior designer David Hundley (who grew up in New Mexico and now works in Beverly Hills), follows these design rules:

- Acquire items that are pure and not too decorative.
- Incorporate items indigenous to the area.
- Choose the color you're looking for.

LEFT: Modern and contemporary furnishings make an ideal complement to historic Southwestern architecture. Here, interior designer David Hundley stacks and elevates two wooden trunks on a steel base. Made in the 1930s, the unusual turquoise blue trunks are lined with tin to keep the rodents out. FAR LEFT: In Bill Farmer's home, southwestern antiques often lend an air of austere simplicity. Here, an eighteenth-century Peruvian ranchero chair sits in front of an old Mexican table painted blue. The ornate gilded wall mirror is typical Spanish Colonial design, while the Renaissance plate hanging on the wall is an Italian reproduction. BOTTOM LEFT: An intricately carved seventeenth-century Jacobean bench anchors this hallway. Cross collection includes sixteenth-century Spanish to contemporary items. Carved door is East Indian from Seret & Sons (see Sources). BOTTOM FAR LEFT: Glenna Goodacre, noted sculptor who designed the powerful Vietnam Women's Memorial in Washington, D.C., leans towards eclectic, European styling in her Santa Fe house. Here, Mexican antique doors lead to her study. Sitting atop the old Dutch chest is a collection of old frames. Above the chest is a painting of a Portuguese farm scene.

PART TWO

Regions

RIGHT: **This steeply pitched Territorial-style cottage in San Antonio houses "Horse of a Different Color," an eclectic antique shop owned by collector Fred Pottinger, who often uses the shady portal for evening dinner parties.** OPPOSITE: **Supple vines wound into the shape of the state of Texas hang on a wooden fence.**

West Texas

"I was born upon the prairie where the wind blew free and there was nothing to break the light of the sun. I was born where there were no enclosures and where everything drew a free breath."

—TEN BEARS, YAMPARIKA COMANCHE

WHEN THE TRANSCONTINENTAL RAILROAD FIRST CROSSED THE U.S. IN THE 1870S, the definition of what was Southwest followed the tracks. By 1880 it reached every section of Texas, thereby designating the Lone Star State as the easternmost gateway to the sparsely settled region. Today, west Texas can still be classified as part of the American Southwest, for its history, landscape, and architecture make it so.

❂ The Edwards Plateau east of the Pecos River has an especially Southwestern feel with its open skies, deeply eroded badlands, and richly colored soil. In the Texas panhandle, just south of Amarillo, Georgia O'Keeffe began painting her sensuous Southwestern landscapes while teaching at Canyon College (now Texas A&M University) near Palo Duro Canyon— the "Grand Canyon of the Red River." By the 1920s, O'Keeffe's muted polychromatic landscapes under intense blue skies had become the stylized regional image adopted by most Americans.

❂ In the south, starting at El Paso, the Rio Grande winds its way toward Mexico, where it enters the Gulf of Mexico at the city of Brownsville. This river marks the borderland of Texas and Mexico, an area of intense interaction between Latino and Anglo worlds, an interaction that infuses this easternmost region of the Southwest with a culture uniquely its own, a culture we call "Tex-Mex."

❂ The Lone Star State has contributed much to Southwestern architecture and interior design. The prairie ranch house, with its portal stretching pragmatically across the west- or south-facing facade, takes on real Texas charm when appointed with all the accoutrements of "cowboy country."

The Attitude

Cattle country...scattered ranches...wide-open spaces... tumbleweed somersaulting over a vast plain...honky tonks: This is Texas. In some places the frypan flat plain stretches away forever. West Texas is basin-and-range land bounded by the Pecos River in the east and the Rio Grande in the west.

Deep canyons along the upper Rio Grande add to the beauty. This semiarid landscape covered with low scrub (cactus, juniper, mesquite, mountain cedar) is home to wild turkey, mountain lion, bobcat, coyote, and more than a hundred species of snake (at least sixteen poisonous). Before their defeat at the hands of the U.S. Army, several American Indian tribes—Apache, Cheyenne, Arapaho, Kiowa, Comanche—freely roamed the area.

Architecturally, we can thank Texas for giving us the prairie ranch, built of local stone or wood, with a deep portal offering respite from heat and blazing sun. Built by fiercely independent homesteaders, these practical one-story cottages still dot the landscape of west Texas. That fierce independence lingers, too. Proud Texans make their own way; some ranchers even generate their own electricity with on-site windmills.

Pockets within the west Texas landscape still contain picturesque historic villages. Fredericksburg, in hill country, has special charm. Here, German pioneers dug limestone from the nearby hillside to build houses that reminded them of home. In the past ten years the town of 7,000 has undergone considerable gentrification earning it the moniker "The Santa Fe of Texas."

Thanks to Texas we have "cowboy country," a stand-alone design style featuring rugged fabrics, leather upholstery and lampshades, and the crafts of tooling, wattling, and whittling. Cowboy country offers a whole new palette of materials—deer antlers used for door pulls, horseshoes sculpted into garden arches, bones made into drawer pulls. Rugged design elements include Beacon blankets, chunky wooden furniture, and Navajo rugs. Closer to the Mexican border you'll find colorful pottery, brightly hued serapes, and elaborate punched tinwork.

ABOVE: **The Gage Hotel in Marathon, Texas, has a pure southwestern feel to it, with its adobe walls, projecting vigas, shady portal, turned porch posts, and central courtyard.** LEFT: **An old cupboard *sans* doors houses a picturesque collection of French, English, and Mexican pottery and gourds in this San Antonio loft kitchen. Giant leaves were painted on the wall with latex. Marble countertop was salvaged from a soda fountain shop; marble sink is a custom design.** OPPOSITE LEFT: **Palo Duro Canyon, outside Canyon, Texas.** OPPOSITE RIGHT: **A dry sink sits beneath a tooled leather mirror in the dining room of Mark Clay's house in Comanche, Texas.**

portfolio
Home on the Range

When pioneers settled west Texas in the mid-1800s, the economy was based on cattle breeding. Population was sparse— less than two persons per square mile. For their "home on the range" settlers often chose a variation of the easy-to-build Territorial-style ranch for its pragmatic design and livability. Most often the one-story, four-room ranch house was built of native stone, a natural insulator. A marvel of self-sufficiency, the 900- to 1,800-square-foot design kept quite cool on blazing hot summer days (with shutters closed to keep out the sun), and stayed cozy warm in winter due to the stone absorbing the sun's heat during the day, then releasing it slowly after sunset. Two fireplaces, one on each end of the floor plan, took the chill off during frosty winters. The pitched tin roof helped out too, reflecting hot summer sun and easily shedding snow in winter.

These prairie ranch designs were extremely well thought-out. Though only four rooms, each was of equal size so the house didn't feel small. When properly sited, prevailing breezes swept through the entry hall from front door to back door creating a natural breezeway. The sun warmed the house as it crossed the sky—bedroom and kitchen in the morning, living and dining rooms in evening.

ABOVE: **The tin-roofed stone prairie ranch on South Austin Street, built in 1881 by James Madison McCrary, is now a Texas historic site.** OPPOSITE: **The portal nestled into the crook of the L-shaped house (added during the Beards' restoration) is a favorite hangout—a curiosity shop of antiques, including a log daybed covered with fabrics and throw pillows.**

RIGHT: **Iron stars (once used as masonry reinforcements) line porch beams, a fitting decorating detail for the Lone Star State. A local blacksmith fashioned three iron arbors from old horseshoes and placed them at each entrance to the house. Wisteria vines cover the arbors in spring and summer.** OPPOSITE LEFT: **A large armoire in the entry hall, flanked by lights made from deer antlers, serves as a hall closet. A collection of custom-made cowboy boots stands at parade rest on the floor.** OPPOSITE RIGHT: **Immediately inside the front door a slipcovered English butler's bench offers a classy touch to the humble chore of removing dusty boots after a ride.**

In settlement days these four-room cottages (with backyard privy) housed a family of seven or more. Mom and dad slept in the only bedroom, while children carved sleeping spaces out of the underused corners in other rooms. Large armoires, wall pegs, and trunks scattered about the house kept the family's clothes and linens.

The smaller version of this design, the "Sunday house," was built by the rancher as a weekend cottage in town. On Saturday mornings he packed up his family, hitched the horse and buggy, and clip-clopped an hour or more to town, trading in the afternoon and attending Sunday morning church services before heading back to the country in time for chores.

The stone prairie ranch featured on these pages is located in Comanche, a small agricultural community 140 miles northwest of Austin. The county was legally created in 1856 with post offices established at Cora, Comanche, and Resley's Creek by 1860.

ABOVE: **Old hickory cane-seated chairs pull up to a simple farm table in the breakfast room.** RIGHT: **In the kitchen, a plain white-painted breakfront holds flea market finds and blue-and-white farmstead china.** OPPOSITE: **The dining room table, a Texas antique, is surrounded by Ralph Lauren "Coty" chairs. The chandelier is made from steer antlers.**

Settlers formed neighborhoods near these sites but none became a real town early. Indians raided regularly, making the frontier a dangerous place. Many original settlers gave up and moved back East. The 1860 census counted 709 citizens in the entire county. Ten years later it had risen by only 300 people. Most of the raiding problem was over by 1870, when the town of Comanche was formally organized. The next year, a dry-goods store opened on the corner of the town square operated by R. P. McCrary and his two sons.

R. P. (Reason Pinkney) moved his wife and two sons from Alabama to east Texas in 1868 looking for a fresh start after the Civil War. Both R. P. and his eldest son, James Madison McCrary, fought in the Confederate army, and the family suffered economically during Reconstruction. In 1870 they moved to Comanche where James paid forty-five dollars for property on a corner of the town square and opened a general store— R. P. McCrary & Sons—carrying dry goods, groceries, hardware, lumber, saddle and harness, drugs, furniture, and jewelry. (Later R. P. built the county's first cotton gin.) Everyone in the family helped run the store, and lived in the back. Soon after setting up shop in Comanche, James looked up the Griffith family, whom he had known in Arkansas a few years before.

Two stone fireplaces heat the cottage. This one is in the bedroom where a Western revival bed with tooled-leather headboard and footboard sits on old plank flooring covered with skins and rugs.

"He was particularly interested in locating Miss Ella Griffith, who was living with her aunt and uncle in their log home on Sweetwater Creek," writes Sharon Ray, James' great granddaughter, in The Comanche Chief. "As the story goes he found Ella wading in a stream, and she was quite embarrassed that he caught her barefooted. They married a year later. Ella was only fourteen years old; James was twenty-seven. He wanted to wait until she grew up before they married, but because she was an orphan, he decided to marry her and take her home for 'his mother to raise.'"

At first the newlyweds lived in the back of the store, where their first two children were born. Then in 1876 R. P. died suddenly from a blow to the head with an axe handle during a fight. His assailant was never convicted—he hanged himself in the town jail before going to trial. James took over the family store.

With a third child on the way, living quarters in the back of the store were tight. James decided to start construction on the lot he had purchased on South Austin Street a month before marrying Ella. James did much of the work himself, hiring a stone mason to help build the one-story, L-shaped structure out of native rock. Eighteen-inch stone walls made for a sturdy structure, and a long time building. Finally, three years and a third child later, the family moved into the partially built house along with a niece and James' widowed mother. James and Ella raised eleven children in that little rock house. Most survived; one died in childhood. Another died from the same flu epidemic that killed Ella in 1920. James continued to live in the house alone until his death in 1932, when the property passed into the hands of his heirs.

For fifty-five years the house sat empty, looking like an old friend in mourning, becoming more decrepit as years passed. Gradually, it fell apart from neglect. Then, in 1987, Tyler and Teresa Beard discovered the little stone house, an orphan covered with brush. The couple, both native Texans, were fleeing the fast life of high-powered jobs and international travel. "Enough," they said. "Let's return to our roots." So they rented an RV and drove five thousand miles covering the Southwest and all the areas of Texas they thought they might like. While driving through Comanche they stumbled on McCrary's dilapidated old cottage and immediately fell in love with its potential, despite its condition. At least 50 percent of the building lay in a heap on the ground. One end was completely gone. Trees literally grew through the floorboards. The Beards bought it and set about restoring both the house and the surrounding five acres of pasture with a creek in the back and a gnarled old mesquite tree that once made it into Ripley's Believe It or Not. "We both love the historical past of art and architecture and feel Texas needs to preserve everything she has," Tyler explained. "It is a great feeling to save a piece of history."

"It took the better part of a year," Teresa adds. "Six months on the actual house, six months on the grounds." To save money, the couple did the no-brains work and a lot of cleanup, hiring subcontractors at major stages to do intricate, detailed jobs.

They replaced all floorboards, laid recycled brick pavers in the kitchen, added the rear portal, carved bathroom space out of the kitchen, restored beadboard ceilings, and custom built a large kitchen sink from pine. As a reminder of place, they installed "Indian shutters," heavy wooden interior shutters that close the place up tight. "It was something we saw in lots of old houses," Teresa explains. "When Indians attacked, homesteaders pulled their shutters closed barricading themselves inside. The shutters also help keep out hot sun."

ABOVE: **Leather boot-stitched club chairs flank the living room fireplace. On the pine mantel Navajo baskets mix with tramp-art frames and well-worn children's cowboy boots.**

OPPOSITE: **New furniture from the Ralph Lauren collection mixes well with primitive antiques, such as the weathered cupboard in a corner of the living room.**

The Beards built a barn on the property and started collecting authentic Texas antiques and memorabilia from pioneering days under the name True West Design. They soon found an unquenchable market for their treasures—fancy restaurants, theme parks, Hollywood movie sets. It wasn't long before they outgrew the little house on South Austin Street.

About the time they decided to sell the property they met Mark Clay, creative director with the Ralph Lauren Home Collection in Dallas. One night over supper he made the first offer. "The simple honesty of the place attracted me," he says. "Rough-hewn stone walls, brick and wood floors, plain shuttered windows—it's refreshingly unmodernized comfort, a perfect place for living the simple life." Mark lives in the house weekends and holidays, a cherished respite from his fast-paced Dallas job.

An expert at interior design, Mark mixed his own prize treasures with furniture, fabrics, and household goods from the Ralph Lauren Serape Collection and from True West Design, creating a masterpiece of cowboyana.

It's a difficult tightrope to walk. The danger of stepping over into western kitsch lurks about every decision. Judicious use of antiques and authentic fabrics keeps the danger at bay, creating a lovely setting for a comfortable small-town life.

"It's an evolution," Mark advises. "You don't just go out and shop for a room. I had been buying for years, going to antique shows and yard sales, digging up things in my grand-parents' garage."

ABOVE: **A twigwork desk made by a local craftsman is a study in efficiency.**
OPPOSITE: **Upturned horseshoes decorate the panels of this Mexican sideboard where Mark keeps his stereo. Upturned horseshoes are good luck; when turned down all the luck runs out.**

RIGHT: A rustic twig gate leads to the Santa Fe-style casita—two suites with luxurious bathrooms heated by the sun. OPPOSITE: A beehive-style ruin near Moab, Utah.

Four Corners

"Here you may yet find the elemental freedom to breathe deep of unpoisoned air, to experiment with solitude and stillness . . . to make the discovery of the self in its proud sufficiency which is not isolation but an irreplaceable part of the mystery of the whole."

—EDWARD ABBEY ON THE COLORADO PLATEAU

FOUR CORNERS, U.S.A.—THE ONLY PLACE WHERE FOUR STATES TOUCH EACH OTHER. Utah, Colorado, Arizona, and New Mexico come together at right angles here, near the eastern end of the mile-high Colorado Plateau. Two American Indian reservations (Navajo and Ute) also abut each other, the tribes living peacefully side by side. Even today, the area is sparsely settled and geologically magnificent, home to myths, dreams, and endless adventure.

○ In this red-rock and blue-mesa country, far from any interstate highway, the morning sun lights a pink and orange wilderness of erosion—sheer snow-covered peaks formed by volcanic eruptions, stunning pink canyons and ridges carved by glaciers and streams, fantastic red sandstone arches, towers, and bridges carved by water and wind over a period of 150 million years. The area is famous for its ruins of an ancient civilization—the Anasazi, who, in the thirteenth century, carved villages out of limestone cliffs two thousand feet above the valley floor, and foraged for food amid the desert scrub. One hundred years later they left hurriedly and inexplicably, leaving behind jewelry, mugs, weapons, and pots of corn. Evidence of their existence abounds throughout the area in ruins of their dwellings and cryptic petroglyphs carved into stone.

○ Architecturally, the Four Corners is responsible for giving us the kiva (whose importance to Southwestern architecture cannot be underestimated), and the classic gold rush cabin built of logs.

The Attitude

The Four Corners symbolizes the cradle of U.S. civilization, the place where the Anasazi (an ancient nomadic people migrating from Alaska in 3,000 B.C.) built permanent houses and settled, for they had found the perfect climate—300 yearly days of sunshine, and reliable winter supplies cascading out of the snow-capped mountains. They derived sustenance by hunting and gathering their food—fish, rabbits, deer, piñon nuts, juniper berries, prickly pear, wild greens. By A.D. 800—while Europe was languishing in the Dark Ages—the Anasazi had become remarkably sophisticated, cultivating corn, squashes, and beans, which together form the foundation of a healthy, well-balanced diet.

Southwestern architecture is rooted in the pit house, the Anasazis' first home when they became a settled, agricultural society. Simple and remarkably efficient, these underground chambers (often accommodating several households) began with a crude pit dug a few feet into the ground, usually on mesa tops but occasionally in cliff recesses. They plastered inside walls with mud; laid a timbered roof sup-

ported by four main corner timbers; fashioned a central hearth, partitions, and storage bins; and finished it with a *sipapu*, or hole in the floor, symbolic entrance to their spiritual underworld.

In Mesa Verde the people lived in pithouses from about A.D. 550 to 750, when they began building apartments above ground with upright walls made of poles, stone, and mud, using adjacent pithouses for food processing, tool manufacturing, and rituals. The kiva, in the Pueblo Indian tradition, evolved from the pit house. Anasazis used kivas much as we use churches today— to conduct healing rites or to pray for rain, luck in hunting, good crops.

You can view the ruins of ancient kivas and cliff dwellings (most built from the late 1190s to the late 1270s) in several protected areas of the Four Corners region: Mesa Verde and the Ute Mountain Tribal Park in southwestern Colorado, Canyon de Chelly in northeastern Arizona, Hovenweep on the Utah/Colorado border, and Chaco Canyon and Bandelier in northern New Mexico. Cliff dwellings range in size from one-room

houses to villages of more than two hundred rooms, many plastered on the inside and decorated with painted designs.

Later tribes—the Ute, Pawnee, and Navajo—passed through the Four Corners, claiming the land by the 1600s. Around the same time Spanish explorers discovered the area, leaving their mark upon the culture. Then, with the gold rush in the 1850s and '60s, the area boomed. The railroad built bridges over chasms and blasted tunnels in mountainsides to provide service to miners who were churning out millions of dollars in gold and silver. As the boom continued and money flowed out of the mountains, prostitution, gambling, and rowdy saloons prospered in this rugged corner of the world.

Today, Four Corners architecture showcases a mixture of cultural influences. In Moab and Durango you'll find spindle-bedecked Victorian cottages alongside Craftsman houses with their tapered piers and large overhanging eaves. Spanish settlements (particularly in the San Luis Valley) have an abundance of one-story stucco houses with arched doorways and clay tile roofs. In rural areas Territorial-style stone, log, and cedar houses are commonplace. You seldom find authentic adobe houses with earthen roofs, but a few still exist. In the mountains of Utah and Colorado, eccentric owner-built, owner-designed dwellings dot the landscape, much as they have for the past 150 years. The metal roof enjoys great popularity here where forest fires can be a problem and snow falls heavily in winter. Local artisans and craftspeople provide a rich supply of American Indian and cowboy furnishings—blankets, baskets, pottery, iron and tinware, rugged doors, chunky furniture, handwoven natural dyed textiles.

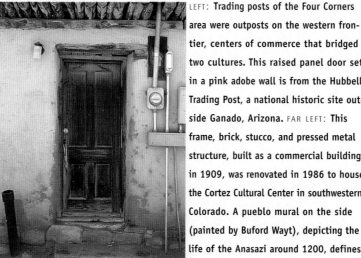

LEFT: Trading posts of the Four Corners area were outposts on the western frontier, centers of commerce that bridged two cultures. This raised panel door set in a pink adobe wall is from the Hubbell Trading Post, a national historic site outside Ganado, Arizona. FAR LEFT: This frame, brick, stucco, and pressed metal structure, built as a commercial building in 1909, was renovated in 1986 to house the Cortez Cultural Center in southwestern Colorado. A pueblo mural on the side (painted by Buford Wayt), depicting the life of the Anasazi around 1200, defines one side of an outdoor plaza used for Navajo and Ute dances during the summer. BELOW LEFT: This modern-day cliff dwelling near Moab, Utah, was hallowed out of a cave left by uranium miners. Plexiglass windows help keep unwanted guests and critters out. OPPOSITE: Rustic twig gates permit access to cottages and lake area at the Blue Lake Ranch outside Durango, Colorado. Twigs are ponderosa pine; posts are cedar dipped in preservative, then buried in the ground.

RIGHT: The main inn, originally a rugged 800-square-feet without plumbing, now encompasses 4,000 square feet and proudly exhibits Victorian embellishments.

OPPOSITE: The Blue Lake Ranch sits on 160 acres in the shadow of the La Plata Mountains in southern Colorado.

Welcome to Blue Lake Ranch

Nestled in a valley of aspen, juniper, piñon and ponderosa pine in the shadow of the La Plata Mountains seventeen miles north of the Arizona/Colorado border, the Blue Lake Ranch typifies the eclectic mix of architectural styles found in the Four Corners area. The hard-to-find bed-and-breakfast sits on 160 acres originally part of the Ute Reservation in the San Juan basin, near the tiny village of Hesperus.

David Alford (who, with his wife Shirley Isgar, currently own Blue Lake Ranch) bought 80 acres of the property with a friend in 1975. "We bought it for five hundred dollars an acre from a Farmington man who won it in a card game," David laughs. The property was homesteaded in the early 1900s by Knute Johnson, a Swedish bachelor who worked at the Hesperus post office. At the time it took a day to get to Durango, now a fifteen-minute trip up the road by car.

In 1910 Johnson, who lived on the property most of his life, built a rustic homestead—three rooms in a 14 x 30–foot clapboard structure, the only heat generated by a coal stove. Over the years Johnson's property sold several times until, in the 1940s, it fell into the hands of Willie LaBatto, an independent cuss with the fortitude to build the three-acre lake now known as Blue Lake. As David tells the story, government officials tried to halt the process but Willie, brandishing a loaded rifle, angrily ordered them off his land. Then he proceeded with his plans, opening the lake to the public for fishing, charging ten cents an inch for fish caught in the pond. Shirley, who grew up on the adjoining ranch, remembers sneaking in with her friends to fish for the huge rainbow and brook trout still found in the lake. LaBatto ran the youngsters off. "We didn't have ten cents," Shirley chuckles.

Today, David and Shirley have doubled the size of those 80 acres, leaving the beautiful blue valley in its natural condition, but adding several cottages and *casitas* which they rent to their B&B guests. It's a quiet, serene location at an altitude of 7,400 feet, an unpolluted atmosphere far, far away from any crowd or traffic jam. Getting the establishment to this point of simple elegance and profitable return has been a labor of love, with emphasis on the labor.

After purchasing the property, David took over the home-stead while his co-owner, Chas Shafer, fulfilled a lifelong dream—building a log cabin with his own hands. It's difficult to tell who had the tougher job. While Chas hauled in massive timbers, David set about renovating the tiny homestead, still without indoor plumbing or running water. He added a green-house, turned the garage into a bedroom, opened up the living room to make it bigger. "I came from Buffalo, New York," he says with a smile. "Being an Eastern boy it was a revelation to move to the West. It was heaven."

In 1980 David bought out his friend and, with his first wife, turned the old homestead into the first bed-and-breakfast estab-lishment in the area. "It all began with one room," he recalls. "In those days it was a homestay. We lived upstairs and rented out a little room on the main floor."

LEFT: **The mansard-roofed yellow barn, renovated with Victorian touches, contains two suites.** OPPOSITE: **One of the ranch's many gardens thrives at the base of the La Plata Mountains.**

From there the establishment continually grew. David built a barn, transformed the old attic into a second guest room, added another bedroom at the end of the house. When the couple was expecting their first child they moved into the back of the adjacent barn, replacing the stall doors with French doors and converting the hay loft into two bedrooms.

"We stayed there for quite a while," David says. "I remodeled the front part of the barn and kept some livestock—pigs, chickens, ducks, turkeys, peacocks, milk cows, sheep, goats, llamas." In 1987 he built a small writing studio. Then in 1990 the couple got into the poultry business, raising organic chickens. "As time went on it became a huge undertaking and we decided we couldn't do this ever again. The feathers and the flies and all of that were just obnoxious." So, David transformed the chicken sheds into a gardening shed, workshop, and caretaker's quarters.

After a divorce, David married Shirley, who grew up on the ranch next door, and Blue Lake Ranch grew to encompass 80 more acres. Shirley, a medical doctor who enjoys architecture

almost as much as she loves medicine, set about recreating authentic Southwest styles at the B&B. The couple spent the early 1990s upgrading the buildings—adding bathrooms, laying Saltillo tile, installing Jacuzzi tubs. Then they took a big step and moved off the property. "It was just time," David explains. "We had expanded enough. It was time for us to have a home, so we built our house at the south end of the ranch on some land Shirley's parents had given to us as a wedding present." And they continued building.

Now, the ranch contains fourteen accommodations in several Southwestern architectural styles—each with a beautiful view and its own garden. David started gardening early on, beginning with bulbs and fruit trees—apple, peach, nectarine, apricot, chokecherry, pear. Jam from the fruit of those trees is a staple sold at the ranch every year. Near their house the couple maintains hollyhock and columbine fields, supplying nursery stock for the B&B's gardens and heirloom seed business.

"The views here are really what it's all about," David says. "We try to orient our buildings toward the sun, toward the views, to create a wonderful feeling of bringing the outdoors in."

"I think we're getting better at it," Shirley adds. "The last casita—with magnificent views, big tiled bathrooms, and walk-in showers—appears to be the favorite."

And they continue to build. Currently, a large log lodge with massive stone fireplace is under construction, soon to contain a bustling restaurant and gift shop.

Built with Smartblock (hollow-core foam blocks filled with concrete and ribbed together with rebar), David and Shirley's new house contains an accumulation of Southwest-style architectural details— pediments over doors and windows, tin roof, wrought-iron balcony railing. A wall of R-6 glass faces south, overlooking the La Plata river and admitting warmth from the sun which helps heat the interior in winter. Exterior is Dryvit, a stucco-like material that's easily sculpted and does not fade.

A 2,200-square-foot Territorial-style barn built adjacent to the house in 1997 is a special event facility for the B&B. First-floor windows are manufactured doors. The low maintenance metal roof, from Pro Panel, comes with a seventy-year warranty. Siding is hand-milled board and batten.

BLUE LAKE RANCH ACCOMMODATIONS

- The Victorian-style Main Inn, originally built in 1910, contains 4,000 square feet with four rooms and luxurious baths featuring walk-in showers, skylights, marble sinks, and walk-in closets.
- The classic log cabin on the lake, built in 1976, features 1,800 square feet in three stories, complete with massive "moss rock" fireplace and floors of pine and oak.
- The mansard-roofed 1,600-square-foot yellow barn, renovated with Victorian touches in 1987, contains two suites (mountain view and piñon view).
- The 600-square-foot Cottage in the Woods, built as a writing studio in 1982, has a small kitchen, jacuzzi tub, pine floors, exposed beams, barn sash windows, and a charming, private Monet garden with Giverney-type bench.
- A 2,600-square-foot Craftsman-style bungalow, with trestle wood floors, built in 1998, is "the kind of house women coming West on the railroad wanted," Shirley explains. "A house like they had back East."
- A 2,000-square-foot passive solar Santa Fe–style casita, built in 1999 with two suites, features a ceiling of vigas and latillas, brick floors set in sand, eight-foot-tall windows, and ten-foot-high ceilings.
- The 700-square-foot River House, a Ute hogan built prior to 1900 on the cascading La Plata River, was renovated in 1993. It has an east-facing door, central fireplace, and pine floor.

Each of the accommodations is authentically furnished with natural materials gathered from shops in Durango, Santa Fe, and Mexico. Recycled wood was used to fashion new tables and shutters. Handmade doors are solid wood. Many baths are finished with Travertine marble from Mexico and limestone from Ecuador. Ironwork makes an appearance in curtain rods, andirons, and hardware. And, of course, there are lots of antiques representing two lifetimes of hunting and gathering.

The log cabin at Blue Lake Ranch is isolated in the woods overlooking Blue Lake. It contains two suites rented as one unit—the 800-square-foot main floor with 500-square-foot loft; and a 500-square-foot guest room below.

portfolio

Classic Log Cabin

The three-story log cabin at Blue Lake Ranch, built in 1976, is a Four Corners classic. Native stone serves as the foundation. The massive stone fireplace (designed to store heat and release it slowly when the fire dies out) is made of local moss rock, commonly found in Southwestern houses. Window seats and two decks create an easy transition between indoors and outdoors. Most of the furniture—and all doors—are handmade.

The cabin sits on a hill overlooking Blue Lake, a spring-fed pond filled with trophy brook and rainbow trout. Depending on the season and the weather, coyote, eagles, hawks, owls, mule deer, and elk on their seasonal migrations can be seen feeding at the lake.

A few years ago the cabin was winterized, including rechinking with synthetic caulk that moves with freeze/thaw cycles. So, no matter what the season, it's a cozy, isolated retreat away from the cares of everyday twenty-first-century life.

Exposed logs on the cabin's interior create a homey atmosphere conducive to mountain living. Pendleton blankets from the 1920s and '30s gain new life as curtains and pillows. When combined with colorful Navajo rugs, they create a colorful backdrop in this natural wood interior. Stone fireplace is made of native moss rock. The circular stairway leads to a loft bedroom and bath. Furnishings are a combination of cowboy mountain paraphernalia and Native American crafts.

LEFT: Though tiny, the cabin's kitchen is remarkably efficient. Cabinets are pine with iron hardware. Countertop is inlaid wood of several different types in a geometric design by a local craftsman. Pottery is Talavera from Mexico. RIGHT: Similar materials are found in the loft bathroom (with a Saltillo tile countertop), and elsewhere in the cabin, creating continuity. OPPOSITE: The loft bedroom, with its king-sized bed, has a tongue-and-groove knotty pine ceiling, its own fireplace, and spectacular views of the La Plata mountains.

ABOVE: **Foothills of the Sangre de Cristo Mountains north of Santa Fe.**
OPPOSITE: **Colorful chile *ristras* are commonly found hanging on front doors or posts of Southwestern homes.**

New Mexico

"Elsewhere the sky is the roof of the world; but here the earth was the floor of the sky . . . the thing all about one, the world one actually lived in, was the sky, the sky!"

—WILLA CATHER, FROM *DEATH COMES FOR THE ARCHBISHOP*

NEW MEXICO IS ANCIENT BY ANY STANDARD. Stone Age remains found near Clovis, in the eastern part of the state, show that human beings first entered the area more than 10,000 years ago. The Anasazi culture flourished in the San Juan River Basin in the first millennium A.D. Santa Fe is the oldest continuous seat of government in North America. The Palace of the Governors, built by the Spanish in 1610, is the oldest public building in the nation.

◉ Architectural evidence of New Mexico's colorful history dots the state—from ancient pueblos and kivas to well-preserved Spanish colonial haciendas and plazuelas to remnants of the not-so-distant Wild West—Kit Carson's house and museum in Taos, Fort Sumner where sheriff Pat Garrett gunned down Billy the Kid, the romantic ghost towns of Mesilla and Lincoln in the southwestern and central part of the state, respectively.

◉ Perhaps due to its salubrious climate, New Mexico enjoys a reputation for environmentally sound construction techniques—first as the leader of the solar energy movement in the 1970s, then as the seat of strawbale and rammed-earth construction in the 1980s and 1990s. Today New Mexico is at the forefront of the "green building" movement. Living in this climate, geography, and culture puts people in touch with their environment, proving the old maxim that the closer you get to nature, the less you need.

The Attitude

New Mexico is "the land of enchantment," "the sunshine state," home to Pueblo Indians, descendants of the Anasazi, tamed by Spanish friars and missionaries whose burros crisscrossed the hard, sun-baked earth in the 1600s and 1700s. Forget the clock. Here, it's perpetual *mañana* time; "I'll expect you when you get here" is a common aphorism.

New Mexico has some of the flattest land in the world, and some of the most rugged—from desert basins to snow-capped peaks to unique volcanic formations. Geographically, the state can be divided into three distinct regions. The eastern third is part of the Great Plains, miles and miles of wheat and grazing land for cattle. The long, meandering Rio Grande river bisects the state north to south in the central one-third, beginning in the Rocky Mountains of southern Colorado and opening into the craggy Sangre de Cristo range where it spreads to form a series of broad, peak-fringed basins while winding its way toward the border at El Paso. The western third is high and mountainous with the northwest corner belonging to the Colorado Plateau, spectacular scenery of broad valleys and plains crudely cut by deep canyons and dotted with mesas. The U.S. government claims the inhospitable southern desert (32.4 percent of the state) for its missile bases.

Because of the arid climate, most early settlement occurred along the rivers. By 1300 Pueblo Indians had established eighteen villages along the Rio Grande from Taos south to Isleta, villages that still exist today. A peaceful people, the Pueblos practiced domestic arts—pottery, weaving, home decoration—while raising corn, beans, squash, and cotton for weaving into their blankets. Nomadic Navajo and Apache tribes shattered their serenity in the 1400s, beginning four centuries of warfare between the people.

Spanish settlers arrived in the 1600s, setting up a self-sufficient farming and ranging economy while attempting to convert the Indians to Christianity. The huge territory (which at the time included Arizona and part of Colorado) fell under Mexico's governance in 1821. The annexation of Texas in 1845 included the portion east of the Rio Grande. Mexico ceded the rest (except for the southern strip included in the Gadsden Purchase of 1853) to the U.S. in 1848. In 1853 the territory was divided, establishing the boundaries of New Mexico, Arizona, Utah, and Colorado. New Mexico remained a U.S. territory for sixty-two years. Fearing higher taxes, residents resisted statehood. Congress, at the same time, doubted democracy could work in a Spanish-speaking state. Finally, after the schools began teaching English, New Mexico became a state in 1912.

Thankfully, this long colorful history is documented in New Mexico's architecture. You can still find old adobe pueblos with people living much as they did in olden days; authentic colonial haciendas graciously restored and appointed, and charming rural Territorial houses with steeply pitched roofs and Greek Revival details. One-of-a-kind traditional furnishings, both old and new, are readily available in the many trading posts, boutiques, flea markets, antiques shops, and museums sprinkled throughout the state. Chile ristras in a variety of shapes and sizes can be purchased from roadside vendors almost anywhere you travel.

INSIDER'S TIP *Shopping for authentic American Indian crafts in New Mexico is a special treat. Baskets, pottery, weavings, Navajo blankets, and jewelry are abundant. For a good variety, trading posts around Santa Fe, Albuquerque, Chimayó, Taos, and Gallup ("American Indian capital of the world") are the best places to shop. Santa Fe holds a flea market just outside of town every weekend during the summer. For the serious collector, the city's Indian Market every August is an event not to be missed.*

ABOVE: **Chimayó is a sacred place for both Hispanics and Tewa Indians.** TOP: **Santuario de Chimayó, classic adobe mission architecture in northern New Mexico. On Good Friday, thousands of Hispanic and American Indian pilgrims walk to this tiny church, some hiking great distances.** LEFT: **This Pueblo-style adobe house, one of the oldest in Santa Fe, boasts viga ceilings, four-poster beds, cast-iron furniture, and angelic figurines.** OPPOSITE: **Foothills of the Sangre de Cristo Mountains.**

portfolio
Mud Hut Redux

More than a beauty, it's art. An outcropping, really, looking like part of the land, part of the Magdalena mountains beyond. Nicknamed "The Mud Hut" because of its honest-to-god adobe construction, yet tongue-in-cheek because, at 3,500 square feet, it's far from a hut. "What I'm most proud of," states architect Anthony Anella, "is how the house fits into the landscape. The forms of the house echo the forms of the mountains in the distance. The details resonate with the cultural context."

The Bosque Del Apache National Wildlife Refuge, which attracts literally hundreds of thousands of waterfowl each winter, is the primary reason for locating on this remote six acres of mesquite- and creosote-covered desert adjacent to the Rio Grande Valley. That and The Owl Bar in nearby San Antonio, a state institution, home of the best greasy green-chile cheeseburger in the world.

Raymond Plank, founder and CEO of Apache Oil Corp., uses his Mud Hut as a winter retreat, a warm-weather respite from the winds, snow, and cold of Wyoming, his primary residence. In 1990, Plank hired Anella to help design and build a vacation house where he could entertain while maintaining his privacy. Anella conceived a hacienda-style plan with two wings— a private master bedroom wing on the east incorporating a large bedroom and bath and a spacious living room; and a larger, more public guest wing on the west consisting of two guest rooms, two studies, and large dining room/kitchen.

LEFT: **Hand-plastered mud walls give the interior a soft, undulating surface with a wonderful texture. Remnants of straw are still visible in this dining room wall.**
OPPOSITE: **An eight-foot-wide portal facing the central courtyard admits morning sun into the guest wing, while providing afternoon shade. While massing of the house has a modern feel to it, all the Spanish Colonial details are present—wood beams, corbels, and posts.** FLOOR PLAN: **Contemporary version of hacienda floor plan, designed by Anthony Anello.**

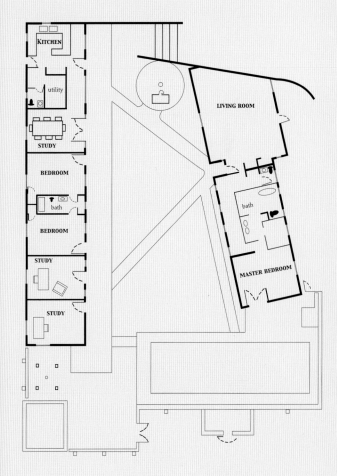

The two wings are actually separate buildings, each with its own foundation and roof, yet tied to each other by a surrounding adobe wall (in the Spanish Colonial tradition) and facing each other across a central courtyard (see floor plan, previous page). Guests come over to the living room for cocktails in the evening while the host visits the guest wing for breakfast and dinner.

Completed in 1991, the Mud Hut is a modern Spanish hacienda with a central courtyard, but instead of four enclosed wings surrounding the courtyard, it has two. Taking the place of the other two wings are a high adobe wall on the highway side, and a lap pool with surrounding low wall on the south side. Entrance to the compound exists through a slot where the walls overlap—a cornstalk gate denoting the threshold between the natural and the man-made landscape.

Behind the walls the courtyard opens to the south and to the sun encompassing a desert garden, lap pool (off the master bedroom), working windmill (a 1932 Chicago Aeromotor with a rustic wood structure, original to the site), and an outdoor eating area recalling the design of a kiva, complete with firepit and wind deflector. The wind deflector corresponds in mass to a fountain by the pool, helping to center the courtyard.

Structurally, the Mud Hut has load-bearing, sun-baked adobe walls and ponderosa pine beams. Stucco covers the exterior while interior walls are hand-finished mud plaster. Hot water pipes installed in the subfloor warm Saltillo tile flooring, thus radiating healthful heat throughout the house. All windows and doors are wood. To obtain light-filled interiors, Anella placed clerestory windows high in the walls of the master bedroom and bath, kitchen, and both studies.

LEFT: Square wood ceiling beams project onto the exterior, much like traditional vigas in Pueblo-style architecture.
OPPOSITE ABOVE: On the exterior, four different colors relate to different aspects of the natural landscape. The reddish color of the west wing relates to the river side of the site—salt cedar, cottonwoods, and willows. The curved east wall has a purple tinge reminiscent of the purple-colored bark of the four-wing saltbush dotting the desert. The bodies of the house sections match the color of the ground, while the mass of blue-gray chimney echoes the sky.
OPPOSITE BELOW: An iron cornstalk gate at the point where the two surrounding walls meet allows entrance into the central courtyard as well as the hacienda-style house.

portfolio

Strawbale Love Story

In the beginning it was an attraction of opposites—Jim Wakeman, an environmental engineer, a pragmatic, linear thinker drawn to mathematical solutions, and Noël Bennett, painter, weaver, author, possessed by a keen aesthetic and a poetic sensibility. The two collaborated on more than the business of living. They often made sculptures together. But no sculpture was so monumental as the designing and building of Vallecito, their experimental strawbale project in remote northern New Mexico, testament to their courage, environmental integrity, and devotion.

ABOVE: **Size of the stuccoed columns was determined by the dimensions of stacked strawbales that surround a load-bearing post.** LEFT: **Inside aesthetics harmonize hard and soft surfaces. Spanish bancos ring the living space. Fabrics are hand-woven cotton, mostly from Indonesia and Guatemala. It's a simple palette using few materials, thereby enhancing the feeling of space and continuity.**

The principles guiding Vallecito started in Cathedrals Canyon, a fragile natural amphitheater in northern New Mexico crammed with sheer rock spires. After Jim and Noël purchased the property in the early 1980s, they built a contemplative retreat—a structure to protect humans from nature and nature from humans. "The land was fragile and beautiful. It was critical that construction be done gently, with the utmost care the human spirit could muster," Noël explains.

Such a pristine area called for the smallest footprint possible, so the couple confined themselves to a tiny three-inch damage margin around the building envelope allowing them to place one foot sideways outside the structure to hammer overhead. Jim even devised a tramway up the steep hillside to haul materials to the site without touching the ground.

That project plunged the couple deeper into the subject of ecological building. Reading Bill Devall's book *Deep Ecology* introduced them to the concept of metanoia. In the book, Devall uses the word metanoia to describe a fundamental transformation of mind or character (in contrast to intellectual knowing), a spiritual conversion necessary to effect true environmental change.

Armed with a grant from the National Endowment for the Arts, Jim and Noël began to research and write a book on gentle building for fragile natural areas. Titled *A Place in the Wild*, the book began with three unalterable criteria. An environmentally responsible structure must have:

(1) Minimum visual impact—it fits the site, blends into nature.

(2) Minimum physical impact—it confines itself to areas of prior human impact, or is pared to essentials and inlaid into native vegetation.

(3) Minimum environmental impact—it employs non-toxic, sustainable materials, and promotes human living patterns which respect and protect the surrounding natural setting.

Carol Anthony's walled strawbale cloister contains a small studio (left), and tiny thatched santuario (above), a one-room island "with a hat" detached from noise and hurry. Both are surrounded by a low adobe wall, creating a compound. The santuario doorway is a "magic carpet" creation—a mere three-and-a-half feet tall, demanding physical flexibility and a bit of bravery on the part of each entrant.

Enchanted Cloister

For artist Carol Anthony life and art are one. She lives and works in a mystical land of her own creation, an oasis of calm without another house in sight, surrounded by sagebrush, aspen trees, and grama grass on a dusty five-acre plot in Arroyo Hondo outside Santa Fe. In this timeworn spot in the shadow of "Twin Mountain Peaks" (part of the Sangre de Cristo range), she maintains her cloister—a charming walled garden embracing a strawbale studio and thatched santuario, a two-horse manger and, down the hill a ways, her strawbale casita. Gardens and shrines dot the property—sacred places because Carol honors them as such. "This land is my inspiration," she whispers into the wind.

Dedicated to meaningful experience, Carol blithely skirts the mundane and teeters on the edge of convention. Though she lives by herself she is definitely not alone on this slice of land punctuated by washed-out arroyos and dotted with juniper, chamisō, and piñon. Birds, insects, lizards, her many dogs (all rescues), the canopy of stars, the plants, and the planets keep her company, waking and sleeping.

Carol, fifty-six, her twin sister, Elaine (also an artist), and their brother, Jack, grew up in a "crazy, loving family of artists, musicians, and cartoonists" in New York City and Greenwich, Connecticut. Their father, Jack Murray Anthony, was creative director for Young and Rubicam advertising agency for thirty years and (in the late '20s and early '30s) a cartoon contributor to *The New Yorker, Colliers,* and *Punch* magazines. Their mother came from a musical family and sang in a trio with her sisters. "We were fortunate," Carol says wistfully.

Carol left the bustling East Coast in 1992, packed her belongings in a jeep and U-Haul truck and moved to Santa Fe. There she created her own reality, a slice of eighteenth-century life frozen in time. "I've worked hard for my choices and freedom in life," she explains. "Now I give myself permission to recede to nineteenth- and eighteenth-century beingness, but with modern thinking and feelings about fairness and nonjudgment and empowerment."

Searching want-ads and dealing with realtors finally yielded the perfect piece of ground for cerebral isolation—a former ranch of wild grass, rock, and deep arroyos divided into five- and ten-acre parcels, where energy and mystery dance a slow dance. It was the piñons—clumps of big, beautiful mature trees partially shading the dusty desert—that sold her on this place.

That, and the cutglass quality of clear, prismatic sunlight blessing the land much as the shaft of light blesses the inner rooms of Carol's paintings.

Carol set about building her walled garden first, encompassing a studio and thatched hut. "This was the first thing I needed to do, a rite of passage if I'm going to live and be in the West," she explains. "It's my version of all the monastic gardens I've sat in in Europe. I'd immediately go to the monastery in any village I visited, to breathe in all the different levels of silences and plants and trees."

For her building site she chose an ancient space between four beautiful piñons overlooking a clear meadow at the base of the mountains. Then, with the help of "friends, some great humor, tequila, and now and then—hugs, money, and some delicious ratatouille," she constructed her cloister out of strawbales and adobe. "For me, straw and mud and sunshine all equal pure religion," she sighs. "The land, the sky, and the feel of hard work and people working together with their hands and hearts all add up to that brand of life experience that nourishes the soul for years to come."

Completed in 1992, the small compound is Carol's version of a cloister gone Southwest—with hard-carved corbels, old vigas and latillas, ancient windows and doors purchased in Santa Fe but imported from Mexico, Morocco, and India—a quiet, peaceful, magical place complete with outdoor fire circle for cooking and singing. Here, in her tiny, monastic strawbale studio equipped with only a bed, chair, desk, wood stove, and wee icebox, she sat quietly everyday to write and paint, saving up her money (augmented with funds from her brother) to build a casita, a small house complete with bathroom and kitchen.

Antique baby clothes, family heirlooms passed down through three generations, hang from a rope clothesline in Carol's bedroom.

ABOVE LEFT: **A Firebird wood stove heats the tiny strawbale studio. Painting on the wall is a Connecticut landscape Carol completed before moving West. Furnishings are from Nomads (see Sources) and Mexico.** BELOW LEFT: **Desk in Carol's strawbale studio. Painting on the wall is from her father's collection of American primitive art. Windows, shutters, and doors are all reclaimed footnotes of an ancient life forgotten.** OPPOSITE: **Carol chose to keep her studio interior dark, preferring the sharp contrast between sunny desert and cool, nurturing interior spaces. Walls are primed Sheetrock, hand-plastered with a mixture of mud and straw. The floor, too, is a combination of dirt from her land and water covered with Damar varnish to resemble the tint of cow's blood in traditional New Mexican mud floors.**

CAROL'S CASITA

Carol's casita is now a reality—1,600 square feet built by an artisan specializing in unique dwellings. Modeled after the Spanish hacienda style, with a courtyard garden and quiet chapel dedicated to the memory of her twin sister, the house features a ceiling of vigas and latillas, a painted cement floor, and undulating walls with straw peeking through mud plaster. She chose an ancient palette—dark mottled colors, dimly lit rooms—which combine to create a physical inner sanctuary. Strawbales not only define the thickness and strength and curves of the walls, they also lend an old-fashioned warmth and early Southwestern architectural feel.

Nine years on this land have given Carol time to create the mystical desert of her dreams. Crooked branches of wisteria house nests of birds that return year after year. French honeysuckle, looking old and immediately wild, sprout a riot of sweet-smelling blossoms. Tendrils of Concord grapes yield a humble harvest for grazing. Indigenous flowers and herbs weave patterns in the breezes—several sages, spikes of lavender, golden yarrow, now and then some blue salvia. Her small orchard nurtures pears, a handful of apples, and apricots. In the fall, Russian olive trees shimmer gray and green and aspens twinkle with gold.

Carol honors this spot of land where geckos guard the gardens and dogs lie in the sun. "It takes time and quiet and mindfulness for one's spirit to align itself to the soul and the structure and the maintenance of the land one is lucky enough to maintain for a while," she offers. "Like Willa Cather said, 'We come and go, but the land is always here. And the people who love and understand it are the people who really own it— for a little while.'"

ABOVE: A metal bench inside the front door offers a place to sit while pulling on and removing boots, or chatting with a friend. The nicho was built into the straw bales. LEFT: An ornate wooden arch from India greets visitors immediately inside the front door. The painting formerly hung in the stable where Carol's horse stepped on it once after it fell, leaving ghostly horseshoe impressions. OPPOSITE ABOVE: A symbol for unity is carved into the handmade front door. OPPOSITE BELOW: Front facade of Carol's strawbale casita.

LEFT: **Though small, the partially open kitchen is functional and efficient.** OPPOSITE FAR LEFT: **Open shelving showcases Carol's dishes and utensils, a delightful assortment of natural materials in earthen colors.** OPPOSITE ABOVE: **Carol purchased this old Belgian stove in Greenwich Village in the early 1970s when Belgian homemakers literally gave them away, favoring American Wonder Bread over their own creations. Pitcher and bowl are from her father's collection. The round Moroccan vessel holds her sister's ashes.** OPPOSITE BELOW: **Food art, both in painting and in tangible reality, decorates every corner of Carol's kitchen.**

ABOVE: **In the dresser corner hangs a photograph by Katherine Walker, and a painting by Nicolas Carone.** LEFT: **Carol's ample living room belies its small square footage. Her working studio is behind the metal screen decorated with a cross by Santa Fe artist Ford Ruthling. The copper codfish sculpture is a weathervane from her father's collection of American primitive art. Flooring is scored and painted cement.**

RIGHT: **Completed in 1797, the Mission of San Xavier del Bac is one of the finest examples of Spanish mission architecture in the U.S. Plaster covering the structure dries white in the sun, earning the church the nickname "White Dove of the Desert." It dominates the desert high on a hilltop nine miles south of Tucson on the 2.84-million-acre Tohono O'odham Indian Reservation.**

OPPOSITE: **Palatki Ruin in Sedona.**

Arizona

"From my eternity to yours, at this place where our paths cross, I reach out in spirit and thought. I wave my hand in the age–old gesture of greeting, I smile a smile of recognition and say, 'Dear human brother, Dear human sister, so you've come up to here.'"

—HOPI GREETING

THOUGH THE LAST OF THE LOWER FORTY-EIGHT STATES TO BE ADMITTED TO THE UNION, Arizona has a long history. Strong evidence suggests humans have lived here for more than 25,000 years. Dinosaurs walked here, meteors crashed here, a petrified forest and a painted desert exist here—all stark reminders of the wondrous vagaries of the universe.

⚙ In the south is the Sonoran Desert, settled principally by the Spanish in the sixteenth century, a landscape of spectacular monotony. Due to lack of rainfall most everything that grows here has thorns on it, not least of which is the giant saguaro cactus, the sentinel of the desert found primarily around Tucson and Phoenix. The weblike interior skeleton of the saguaro is so strong early settlers used it as a building material, fashioning the ribs into vigas and tools.

⚙ Driving north you discover one mountain outcropping after another after another until you reach the state's mid-section, the agricultural belt, thanks to a massive system of pumps and canals conducting water from the Colorado River. More than three million people live in this most populated section of the state.

⚙ Driving north you climb steadily in altitude through majestic rounded hills, jagged ridgelines, and magnificent Red Rock Country, until you reach a pine forest at Flagstaff at the base of the San Francisco Peaks, western boundary of the Navajo people and home of the kachinas, spiritual guides to the Hopi. This is the entrance to the sprawling fifteen-million-acre Navajo Reservation with Black Mesa, a 5,000-square-mile sandstone platform, ancient land of the Hopi, smack dab in the middle.

The Attitude

Southwestern architecture is not all corbels and vigas. Each region has its own distinct style. In Arizona, that style reflects an intriguing mix of the romantic Wild West, colorful Spanish/Mestizo influences, finely crafted American Indian pueblos and hogans, and ground-breaking "organic" architecture inspired by Frank Lloyd Wright (who moved his school to Scottsdale in 1927) and Italian-born Paolo Soleri who, in 1970, established Arcosanti, a prototypical ecological community north of Phoenix.

In the southern part of the state (around Phoenix, Yuma, Nogales, and Tucson), early architecture consists of adobe and wood-frame ranch-style houses modeled after Mexican churches and haciendas. Local lumber came out of logging mills in Flagstaff. Instead of vigas and latillas, builders used rough-sawn beams and wood rafters. One-by-twelve pine sheathing covered the exterior, capped by a corrugated metal roof.

As mining flourished at the turn of the century, developers built new houses using lumber recycled from old mines—timbers from trestles and bracing for

tunnels shipped by rail from heavy mining areas, like Jerome, Prescott, Tombstone, Patagonia, Clifton, and Bisbee. Meanwhile, optimistic mining towns witnessed the construction of row upon row of wood-frame Queen Anne Victorians with graceful turrets, wrought-iron railings, and wraparound porches built to house bankers and mining executives, while jubilant miners erected neighborhoods of hastily built shacks with little thought for architectural niceties.

In the 1920s and '30s, wood and stone Craftsman-style houses became the rage, nestled in booming neighborhoods amidst plain Sonoran ranches and folk Victorian cottages. In the 1970s and '80s, sprawling free-form houses sprouted up on hillsides around Phoenix and Carefree.

All this diversity adjacent to the largest American Indian reservation in the country, a neomedieval wilderness of semi-independent settlements on a dusty sagebrush and saltbush tableland where traditional hogans sit scattered among aluminum-sided trailers, cinderblock houses, and plain one-story frame boxes.

INSIDER'S TIP *The story of Anglo settlement rests in the quest for mineral wealth, for Arizona is rich in copper, gold, silver, and stone. When gold was discovered in Prescott in 1864, the rush was on. Prospectors attracted miners who in turn attracted merchants, saloon-keepers, clergymen, lawmakers, outlaws, and prostitutes—bringing the white man's civilization to Arizona territory. The romance of the Wild West influenced the state's architecture much more than the Spanish colonial style so prevalent in Santa Fe. Yavapai County alone features more than a dozen ghost towns and mining camps.*

In Prescott today stately Victorian homes, a tree-shaded courthouse square, a picturesque old fort, and charming Whiskey Row provide a mining camp ambiance. Downtown Bisbee, with its lovingly restored historic buildings, has the air of turn-of-the-century San Francisco. The territorial town of Clifton boasts some of the best-preserved Victorian structures in the state. In legendary Tombstone ("The town too tough to die"), the restored 1880s territorial courthouse is a special jewel. While in Tombstone, don't miss the OK Corral, site of the famous shootout between the Earp brothers and Ike Clanton's gang.

OPPOSITE: New adobe construction in the Craftsman style featuring a handmade redwood door and Arroyo Craftsman lighting, located in Sedona, Arizona. ABOVE LEFT: Tramp art and crafts, made during the Depression-era, give character to this Sedona guest room. ABOVE RIGHT: Renovated old adobe ranch south of Tucson, featuring strawbale adobe bancos, raised kiva fireplace, quarry tile flooring, and Mexican eqipale table. RIGHT: Carved and painted double corbel (patterned after corbels that came out of a pueblo in Old Oraibi, an ancient settlement on the Hopi reservation), located in the Colten House in Flagstaff, Arizona (pages 178–183).

portfolio

Sitting on a Gold Mine

It was the angular mining headframe, sitting on a hilltop and made from wood almost a century ago, that drew Bennie Gonzales's eye, beckoning him to purchase the five-acre property in a small development atop Gold Mine Hill outside Nogales on the border with Mexico. During the gold rush the headframe was anchored to cables and used to lower miners in cages down the vertical shaft, as well as to hoist ore out of the mine in buckets. Back then this desert (home to javelina, deer, rabbits, and hawks) was alive with mining activity.

In 1987 Gonzales, a well-known architect who has designed many of Arizona's public buildings, was looking for property to fulfill a dream—designing and building his own home. Both Bennie and his wife, Diane, are painters, so they wanted studio space as well as open loftlike space to exhibit art. "We wanted a house where we could hang paintings and take them down whenever we pleased. A flexible space for just the two of us," he says. "But I also wanted a ranch-style house, more like what I grew up around as a kid in Phoenix in the 1930s."

Bennie, the son of a German-Mexican-Indian father and a French-Irish-Mexican mother, grew up on a twenty-acre farm outside Phoenix in a small house built of one-by-twelve pine with a tin roof and screen porch.

"When I was four, we built an adobe house next door. We used the adobe for the summertime and the frame house for the wintertime," he remembers.

OPPOSITE FAR LEFT: **Old mining headframe on Gold Mine Hill.** OPPOSITE ABOVE AND BELOW: **Steel posts, recycled from a Texas oil field, are rooted five feet in the ground to support the weight of the steel trusses (visible inside) and the metal roof. The surrounding desert supports a few mesquite trees, some palo verdes, and a lot of prickly pear cactus.**

ABOVE: **Siding is rough-sawn one-by-twelve redwood. Bennie salvaged the entrance door from an old Mexican hacienda. Windows come from a 1920s ice plant in Nogales. Steel trusses are similarly recycled.**

When Bennie purchased the property on Gold Mine Hill (formerly a 1,000-acre ranch), the design for his dream house received another jolt of inspiration—the angular headframe looking like some forgotten sculpture standing decrepit and forlorn under the bright desert sky. For Bennie, it was important the house reflect the property's colorful history, a time when Chinese labor brought in on the railroad dug the 150-foot vertical shaft, then tunneled out in several horizontal branches so miners could explore the earth's layers for gold.

The finished 3,000-square-foot house incorporates all of Bennie's design requirements. Post-and-beam construction allows for nonloadbearing interior partitions instead of walls, so they can be easily taken down and reassembled in different locations, changing the floor plan to suit the moment. The living room has traded places with the family room on the opposite side of the house, for example. The bedroom has undergone similar relocation. Two screened porches, on the front and on the rear, serve as his-and-hers painting studios.

Bennie chose a steel framework because it goes up fast, makes a solid structure, and is easy to work with. (As project architect for The Woodlands, a contemporary town outside Houston, Texas, he had used mostly steel framing with wood siding and liked the result.) Pipe column posts positioned outside the structure carry the weight of the roof and the exposed steel trusses visible inside.

The redwood frame, tin roof, and screened porches echo the house of Bennie's childhood, although he added up-to-date insulation and an evaporative cooling system with a pre-cooler attachment so efficient energy bills total less than a hundred dollars a month.

OPPOSITE: Redwood sheathing provides a warm backdrop for hanging art. Diane painted the cow's skull on a sky-blue background. The old saddle was found on the property. The two-foot-tall statue is a copy of an old Mexican figure. LEFT: Even though the galley kitchen is in the center of the floorplan, Bennie gave his wife the kitchen window she requested (only it looks into the interior of the house instead of to the yard outside).

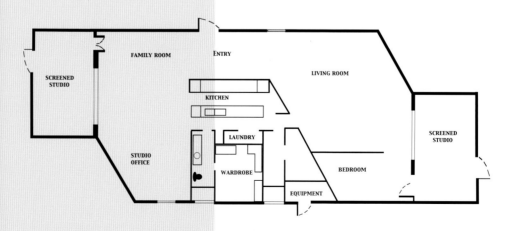

LEFT: **In the main room the ceiling rises to a peak of twenty-four feet. Furnishings are predominantly hand-crafted, playful, and often from south-of-the-border.**
FLOOR PLAN: **Latest incarnation of the Gonzales's floor plan.**

But the most striking design element is the structure's jaunty angularity, close and intimate with the desert on the exterior, yet rising to a peak of twenty-four feet in the grand interior, much like the design of the old mining headframe sitting within view just up the hill. Bennie chose to side the house in wood because, structurally, adobe would have to be reinforced to reach such lofty heights. Wood siding and sheathing was simply more cost effective. The entire construction is capped with a galvanized metal roof painted blue, per instructions from the Homeowners Association governing house design on Gold Mine Hill, though Bennie would have preferred using more historically correct corrugated metal.

Inside, walls are framed with redwood, giving a good surface for hanging artwork. Flooring is concrete finished with ice-cream salt troweled onto the wet surface. The salt dries as it melts and evaporates leaving a pitted surface in the slab. Ceilings have exposed joists for a rough-hewn, camp appearance.

In the end, the house comes off as unpretentious and appealing as the man himself. It was fun to build, Bennie says, because he knew all the contractors. He got the plan approved on a napkin. "Like old-time building in Phoenix," he says with a chuckle. He admits it's not authentic mining camp architecture, "but it's as close as it gets."

portfolio:
Adding Character to a Ho-Hum Tract House

Georgia Bates' modest cinderblock house at the base of Camelback Mountain is typical of many houses built in Phoenix during the early 1960s. It has adobe and brick trim with a stucco finish, and a quaint little courtyard by the front entrance. But one step inside and any similarity with cookie-cutter tract houses ends. You enter a unique realm, a one-of-a-kind creation that smacks of Georgia's impressive personal style. Her favorite piece, after all, is an old Mexican jail door she uses as a headboard for her bed.

"This house is a personal expression of who I am and what I do," Georgia explains. "It's not understood by everyone. I wouldn't call it decorated. It's not trying to be anything other than me."

Though her decorating style is flawless, and her knack for contrast exquisite, it's the juxtaposition of refined Southwestern living with rustic Mexican and Guatemalan architectural antiques that sets the house apart from any others. It makes for a humorous, intriguing, and totally inventive interior.

The owner of Bates' Architectural Collection inherited a love affair with architectural antiques from her father, an artist who designed and built exquisite adobe houses all over the Southwest. The two tramped around Mexico together searching for brick pavers and carved wood doors and posts, orphaned artifacts and odd architectural elements to bring to the States and put into his houses. After her father's death, Georgia decided to carry on where he left off, only with a shop. It's only natural, then, that some discoveries find their way into Georgia's home, making the interior an amalgam of curiosities. She displays the architectural pieces as art, giving them space to breathe and show off their unique details.

TOP: Carved designs on the 200-year-old Mexican bench in Georgia's courtyard have religious significance. OPPOSITE: In the shade of an old palo verde tree, the courtyard of Georgia's house gives a hint of the personality to be found inside. Architectural antiques are found here, as well as inside. The pair of wide-planked 200-year-old *portones* (Mexican doors) put together with *clavos* (bolts) adds a hint of rusticity, along with the early 1800s long bench. Cafe table and chairs are from France. Flooring is kiln-baked adobe brick. Courtyard gate is original to the house.

"I love the history and the aesthetics they can bring into what is otherwise a contemporary setting," Georgia says. "Five years ago, there wasn't any place in Phoenix offering a great collection of Mexican and Guatemalan antiques, so I opened the shop. Most of what I have is between two hundred and four hundred years old. I not only carry pavers, doors, and iron columns, but a nice collection of santos, altars, paintings, and crosses. I see them as folk art or as sculpture, not necessarily as religious icons. The store has some very nice Spanish colonial furniture, as well. It's grown into being more than architectural elements."

When Georgia moved with her daughter to the 2,800-square-foot house in 1992, it was in dreadful shape. Fluorescent green and orange carpet covered the floors, with corresponding colors on the walls. Three different kinds of floor tile converged in a clumsy puddle at the entrance. The tiny kitchen had vinyl-asbestos flooring covered with fluorescent blue indoor-outdoor carpet. Most of the windows had such high sills you couldn't see through them without standing up. How could anyone see beyond such a glare of poor taste?

OPPOSITE: **The simplicity of the sunken living room, with its beehive fireplace, wall of bookshelves, and deeply set window seat, initially sold Georgia on the house.** TOP: **Georgia opened up the wall separating the dining room from the living room, and added an old window unit from a Mexican farmhouse. It's a simple piece consisting of a rustic frame, iron grille, and interior shutters. Dining room chandelier is tin. Leather and ironwork dining chairs are also from Mexico. Table runner is a composite of several Pakistani wedding dresses quilted together and used for dowries.** RIGHT: **The living room window seat is a favorite reading spot. Rare Mexican crucifix is from the late 1700s.**

OPPOSITE: **Georgia designed her iron bed frame to give a feeling of openness to the room, a basic box made to accommodate a standard-sized box spring. An old Mexican jail door, made from sabino wood from the state of Jalisco, serves as a headboard. Tapestry pillow is made from an antique Peruvian rug. Duvet cover is simple white cotton. The antique carved wood door leads to the master bath and takes the place of a "hideous pocket door." Armchair is covered in eighteenth-century Spanish tapestry. Colonial *rapero* (made to store clothing) holds a tiny television.**

TOP: **A beehive fireplace and banco are recent additions to Georgia's master bedroom. Painting on the wall is *Virgin de la luz,* a Mexican creation dating from the late 1780s. The glass-eyed figure standing on the banco is *Christ at the column,* a rare and unique santo carved from wood, painted with gesso, and featuring a sterling silver "crown of light." In the gold frame, *Jesus and the sacred heart,* also dating from the late 1700s.**

The old, established neighborhood with big beautiful trees initially drew Georgia to the site. Once there, three elements sold her on the house, all in the living room—the beehive corner fireplace with floor-to-ceiling bookshelves on one side and cozy window seat on the other. "I'm an avid reader with a massive collection. I found it appalling that every house I looked at didn't have any bookshelves," she says. Once she saw these elements coming together in the living room, she thought she could work with everything else and eventually transform the house into a home. After all, it had good bones and a solid structure.

She bought the house at the top of her price range, so she didn't have much money left for renovation. She immediately tore into those elements she just couldn't abide. She resurfaced and repainted the exterior, then ripped up most of the floor tile, replacing it with Travertine. She couldn't afford to redo the kitchen, so she removed all cabinet doors and stripped the base cabinets leaving an old Mexican finish with remnants of various paints peeking through. After a while she had new cabinet doors made with glass fronts in a simple design to reflect the simplicity of the house. Later, she added a small breakfast nook—an eight-foot-deep bumpout incorporating a large window with a delightful view of the interior courtyard. "The original kitchen was so dark and small and cramped," Georgia says. "It was nice to open it up with windows. Now you feel like you're right in the middle of the garden."

Georgia's favorite project was her bedroom re-do. Like most rooms of the house its windows had high sills. To remedy the problem, She planned a renovation that replaced a window with French doors, then installed a lovely masonry Rumford fireplace (an English energy-efficient design) in the corner.

Now she can lie in bed and see the sun rise, and walk directly to the outdoor swimming pool from her bedroom. With these improvements the modest-sized house feels light and spacious, the plan more cohesive as you walk from room to room. But it still isn't finished. It's a work in progress, and will probably always be so. Next on Georgia's agenda is the master bathroom. "It was added onto the original house, but in a very contemporary format—like Frank Lloyd Wright gone Harley-wrong," she laughs. "There's no way to improve on it other than to bulldoze it down." So, Georgia removed the sliding pocket door and substituted a pair of rustic raised panel doors from Mexico. Until money accumulates to do what needs to be done, she simply keeps the door closed.

DESIGN LESSONS *Georgia's decorating style gracefully blends threadbare primitive with rich elegance. How does she achieve such a seemingly effortless mix? Here are a few of her tips:*

(1) *"The only way to see the beauty of each object—to see its textures, lines, and shadows—is to give it space to breathe."*

(2) *"When designing a room, try to draw the eye from one level to the next—a trick I learned from studying magazine layouts."*

(3) *"Everything is a work of art if you look at it the right way. Something as simple as an old board, or a farm implement, bears the stamp of weather, time, paint, and someone's hands."*

(4) *"Buy only what you love. If you want to start a shop, get a storage van and start collecting as you go."*

RIGHT: **Inviting textures and Mexican antiques beckon from Georgia Bates' guest room in her Phoenix ranch-style house. Walls are drywall with troweled-on texture, then painted Ralph Lauren brown. Bedside *cómoda* is a hundred-year-old Mexican country piece. Carved wood mirror is from the mid-1800s. Acrylic frame over the bed holds a vestment with threads of silk and gold. Colorful Pakistani fabric covers bed pillows. Georgia found the framed bedside portrait of a young woman in a Mexican flea market and fell in love with her "tranquil face."** FLOOR PLAN: **Georgia Bates's 2,800-square-foot, concrete, Sonoma ranch-style house in Phoenix, Arizona.**

portfolio:
Spirited Resurrection

Arizona is known for its Wild West ghost towns, boomtown mining camps suddenly abandoned when the mines shut down. Of these, the most famous is Jerome, the "billion-dollar copper camp" and gold mine, perched precipitously on a steep hillside rising sharply out of the desert two hours northeast of Phoenix. Once dubbed "the wickedest town in America," Jerome grew to be the fourth-largest city in Arizona Territory. The town's raucous growth spawned charming Old-West hotels, trading posts for provisioning, aromatic Chinese restaurants, twenty-four-hour saloons, lively bordellos, a post office built of locally quarried stone, and the fabled Powderbox Church, built entirely of discarded dynamite boxes and mining timbers.

Today, Jerome is an artists' colony and tourist attraction. Several of its old buildings have been fixed up; a few are even completely restored. But the Powderbox Church exists in resplendent glory far beyond the imaginings of its impoverished builders.

TOP: **When the weather is grand, Anne and Tom Gale serve luncheon on the flagstone terrace overlooking the great red rock formations of Sedona forty miles away.** LEFT: **Rear facade of the Powderbox Church in Jerome, Arizona.** OPPOSITE: **Interior of the upper level "sanctuary." Raised platform at the end of the room was for the preacher and the choir. Curtained bed alcoves are placed on either side of the platform. Old French doors open to a small iron balcony. Floors are oak, stained and polished. Walls are plaster. Brass chandeliers are Dutch from the nineteenth century. Chairs are a collection of nineteenth-century Fauteuils covered in simple red/cream cotton toile. When mixed with shabby Oriental rugs and compelling oil paintings from around the world, the result is a surprising combination of refined elegance and primitive rusticity, unexpected and totally charming.**

OPPOSITE: **Weekend forays to junk shops and antique stores in nearby towns yielded magnificent treasures, like this old enamel cast-iron sink with two drainboards, and a large wood-burning Stewart cookstove.** RIGHT: **Today, Anne and Tom Gale are the sole proprietors of Powderbox Church. Originally the heart of a small community, it continues to be a place of fellowship and hospitalilty. On weekends, the couple entertains friends with Sunday brunch, usually inviting twelve to fourteen people. They set the twelve-foot-long table with old blue-and-white Fitzhugh china, antique silver, and starched linens. Overhead, the old iron chandelier is dressed in fresh flowers and greens. The massive green cabinet was a trash-heap find, cast off when the old Jerome Pharmacy closed many years ago.**

The story of the church's construction tells a tale of an early civil rights struggle in the United States. It occurred in 1939, the lean years of the Great Depression. The "white" Methodist congregation uptown forbade Mexican miners and their families (most of whom did not speak English) from worshipping in the sanctuary. Mexicans were relegated to the basement, and otherwise made to feel unwelcome. Under the leadership of Sabino Gonzales (charismatic lay minister, town barber, and a pretty fair carpenter), the Mexicans left and proceeded to build their own church on a rocky promontory in shanty town, where they lived. They wanted a place where they could speak their own language, a place where they were safe from discrimination. Because they were poor, building materials came from whatever they could find—blocks and stones for the foundation, cast-off blasting boxes and recycled trestle timbers for framing.

Despite its humble construction, Powderbox Church (as it was christened) quickly became the heart of the neighborhood. Services were in Spanish, and all were welcome. But the community didn't need a church for long. Not long after construction was completed, Methodists uptown had a revelation.

The congregation walked down the hill *en masse* to the turreted blasting box church and apologized, inviting the Mexicans to come back and worship with them. Incredibly, the Mexicans were happy to oblige. After that, Powderbox Church became a social gathering place used by Mexican families to celebrate weddings and reunions, christenings and wakes. A small cemetery sits on a promontory behind the structure.

When the mines closed in the 1940s, so did Jerome. Most of its citizens departed for greener pastures, selling their household and business possessions to the highest bidder. Mexicans abandoned the Powderbox Church. For a while it became a community theatre. Then, in the early 1950s, when interest in Jerome was at an all-time low, the building was abandoned, left to become a romantic ruin.

Enter George Wiseman and Anne Gale, partners in Wiseman and Gale Interiors, headquartered in Scottsdale. In 1964 the partners, along with Gale's husband, Tom (an architect), bought the building with the idea of restoring it and using it as a weekend retreat, retrofitting it only with historically accurate objects.

"It was in terrible shape," Anne Gale remembers. "Vagrants and tourists had come in and carved their initials. Rude sayings were written on the beaverboard walls. But we liked its spirit. It became a weekend project. Inside, we did a to-the-studs tear-out and started over. Our best friends became the carpenters and plumbers who stayed weekends and helped us work. When you do a job on weekends, it takes forever."

Though the structure was twenty-five years old, no one had bothered to properly finish it. Exterior stucco was still in the gray-colored scratch-coat stage. With help from friends, the new owners stripped the exterior down to its powderbox sheathing (where they found intact labels from the many dynamite companies that supplied the mines in the 1920s and '30s), then replastered in the original gray. They nailed wood shakes to the roof, replaced all windows, and hired a Scottish craftsman to fashion a majestic entry door out of pine. "We wanted to express the nature of the building in its doors," Anne explains. "The front door started with two old Mexican pine doors complete with *postigos*, little iron grille-covered windows we can open and look through, in the Spanish way."

After renovation, the physical layout of the 1,534-square-foot structure remains the same—two large rooms, one on each floor, each thirty-two feet long by sixteen feet wide, including alcoves formed by the four turrets.

Upstairs, the original sanctuary is used as a parlor for conversation and relaxing. Downstairs, the former social hall is a commodious dining room/kitchen. There are three bathrooms, one in a corner of each floor and a third in the belltower over the main entry door. Twin beds tucked into the alcoves and on the mezzanine over the sanctuary provide overnight accommodations for six people.

LEFT: Upstairs, two bed alcoves (each with a twin bed) nestle in turrets on either side of the raised "preacher's" platform. When the red/cream toile curtains are dropped, each guest has a private "roomette." Brass Pullman racks hang on the alcove walls, handy for guests to stow their bags. OPPOSITE: The downstairs bed alcove is closed off from the dining room with a curtain made of vintage hand-blocked linen circa the 1940s. Ladderback chair is an English antique from the 18th century. The round marble table is a French antique. Black Hitchcock chair by the bed sports its original paint. Oil painting is a souvenir from a Russian flea market.

portfolio

The Colton House

Visible for miles away, the San Francisco Peaks dominate the horizon outside Flagstaff, on the edge of the Colorado Plateau. Sacred to both Navajo and Hopi, whose homelands are located nearby, the pine- and aspen-covered mountains reach a peak of 12,670 feet. At their base, at an elevation of 7,000 feet, rests the historic town of Flagstaff, founded in 1880.

Located seventy-five miles from Grand Canyon National Park, Flagstaff has historically been the last stop for provisions before venturing into that great chasm. Though more than 50,000 residents live in Flagstaff, it has somehow managed to maintain its small-town Old West flavor. At the heart of the community is the historic Colton house, home of Dr. Harold and Mary-Russell Ferrell Colton, founders of the Museum of Northern Arizona. There is no disputing the 6,000-square-foot mansion's reputation as one of the most splendid houses in the state, though architecturally it resists classification. In the words of its restorer Edie Blackstone, it's "adventurous, crazier than hell, with a little bit of everything on the inside."

Edie should know, for no one has been as intimately connected to the house since Harold and Mary-Russell died in the early 1970s. Plateau Winds Corporation, Blackstone's historic building restoration and land development company, undertook the one-million-dollar restoration in 1994, bringing the one-of-a-kind structure back to its original state.

But the story begins with the Coltons. Born to wealth and privilege, Harold, a professor of zoology, and Mary-Russell, an accomplished painter, ventured from the luxuries of Philadelphia to the Wild West of the Colorado Plateau, traveling by train, Model T, and sometimes on horseback, to dig through Indian ruins and paint the colorful landscape, often camping under the stars. The lure of the Southwest, its geologic diversity as well as its native cultures, drew them back time after time.

When his father died, Harold inherited a fortune and decided to quit teaching and devote his life to his passion: archaeology of the Southwest. In 1926, Harold and Mary-Russell moved with their two small children to Flagstaff where in 1928 Harold (who had become increasingly concerned over the loss of Arizona's archaeological artifacts to eastern institutions) became a major force in the establishment of the Museum of Northern Arizona, dedicated to the natural and cultural history of the Colorado Plateau. He was later named its first director.

Mary-Russell continued her expeditions into the nearby Painted Desert, and became increasingly interested in the native cultures she found there. The Hopi, in particular, captured her imagination, and she watched with deep regret as their unique arts and crafts declined almost to extinction, replaced by cheap machine-made imitations. Mary-Russell took it upon herself to rescue Hopi arts and crafts, establishing the Indian summer shows at the museum so Hopi, Navajo, Zuni, and Pai artists could display and sell their work. The Coltons' legacy is still alive in the Museum.

LEFT: Flagstaff's historic Colton House, built in 1929, is a crazy quilt of Southwestern styles incorporating Spanish Pueblo Revival and Craftsman bungalow details. OPPOSITE: The spacious living room opens onto the quiet privacy of a small courtyard through French doors with true divided lights. Rough-hewn Douglas fir vigas and aspen latillas form the ceiling.

ABOVE: **This intricately carved built-in pine cupboard is original to the house, as is the frosted-glass wall sconce.**
RIGHT: **The dining room provides space for a large table, seating twelve, made out of alder wood. New Mexican-style chairs are custom-designed to incorporate a cloud motif found throughout the house. The chandelier, too, is custom-designed.**

The family first lived on a farm outside Flagstaff, raising crops, growing a garden, keeping chickens in the yard and a milk cow in the barn. It was a far cry from the luxury of maids and nannies back East, but it was home and the couple worked hard to improve it. Then, eight days before Christmas in 1928, their house burned to the ground. The tragedy made building a new home top priority.

Harold and Mary-Russell had an idea of the kind of home they wanted. Harold, who had some architectural training, drew up a set of rough plans, hiring his brother, a certified Philadelphia architect, to revise and refine them. The couple approved final plans in May of 1929, and construction began soon afterward with specific instructions for builders to use native materials gathered in the vicinity.

It took six months and $60,000 to complete the one-and-a-half-story mansion. When finally finished it was pronounced a work of art, a one-of-kind architectural synthesis of the Coltons' extensive travels throughout the Southwest. More than any other quality, the eclectic blend of three styles—Spanish Colonial Revival, Pueblo Revival, and Arts and Crafts bungalow—is its most unique aspect, resulting in a classic, truly distinguished mansion.

ABOVE: **The first house built in Coyote Springs typifies the architecture, with design details borrowed from the Colton House, including a stone and viga loggia and a cupola atop the roof. Exterior stone is local basalt rock. Arroyo Craftsman lighting carries through an Arts-and-Crafts theme. Radiant hot-water heat, provided by an intricate piping system in the floor and under concrete slabs and sandstone pavers, heats the 4,300-square-foot interior, exterior walkway, garage, and driveway.**
RIGHT: **Inside, a huge "geological" fireplace covering one entire wall depicts the ten strata of rock found in the Grand Canyon.**

COYOTE SPRINGS: MILLENNIAL REVIVAL

On the outskirts of Flagstaff, on the road to the Grand Canyon, sits the Museum of Northern Arizona, founded in 1928, a focus of the art, culture, and science of the Colorado Plateau. The wood and stone Spanish Colonial\Pueblo Revival-style building sits on the edge of a small gorge amidst three hundred acres of mostly undeveloped forest and open-range land. Restoration of the Colton house, the founders' mansion, made it possible for the museum to set aside some of this land for a new community. In cooperation with Plateau Winds Corporation, the development (called Coyote Springs) encircles the landmark Colton House (featured on pages 178–183), creating a residential village divided into nineteen one- to five-acre home sites.

Philosophically, the development embraces the concepts of conservation and preservation creating a setting that blends with nature, rather than confronting it. Home sites were chosen to have the least impact on the landscape, to allow privacy for each house, and to provide unencumbered views of the San Francisco Peaks. Design guidelines stipulate houses must blend with the surrounding environment. Architects deliberately borrow design details from the Colton House—battered exterior walls, building materials of wood and stone, the general scale and feel—giving continuity to the rural community. The entire area is free of fences, allowing wildlife to roam at will.

Sources

Texas

FURNITURE

El Paso Imports, 311 Montana Ave., El Paso, TX 79902; (915) 542-4241, fax (915) 577-9660. In Dallas, 4524 McKinney Avenue, Suite 102, Dallas, TX 75205; (214) 559-0907, fax (214) 559-0901. In Houston, 2431 Dunstan (Rice Village), Houston, TX 77005; (713) 807-9559, fax (713) 807-9595. In Austin, 6415 Burnett Rd. #A, Austin, TX 78757; (512) 458-2000. In San Antonio, 5154 Broadway, San Antonio, TX 78209; (210) 930-4699. Quality primitives and reproductions from the Mexican countryside.

El Paso Saddleblanket, 601 N. Oregon, El Paso, TX 79901; (915) 544-1000. Huge downtown wholesale warehouse featuring rugs, blankets, artifacts, antiques, skulls, baskets, cowboy collectibles, kachina dolls, horn furniture.

Galleria San Ysidro, 801 Texas Ave., El Paso, TX 79901; (915) 544-4444. Sixty thousand square feet of decorative art and architectural elements imported from Mexico, Asia, and Africa. Custom designed furniture and ironwork. Will deal in quantity for commercial applications.

Horse of a Different Color, 140 W. Sunset Rd., San Antonio, TX 78209; (210) 824-9762. Southwestern and Mexican antiques, santos, and collectibles. Source of rare Mexican bultos.

Prairie Rose, 3404 Camp Bowie Blvd., Fort Worth, TX 76107; (817) 332-4369. A mix of ranch, lodge, prairie and western furniture, accessories and antiques. Interior design services available.

Rustic Style, 414 E. Main, Fredericksburg, TX 78624; (830) 997-6219. Unique home furnishings, local custom-made furniture and accessories. Collectibles and one-of-a-kind antiques. Interior design services available.

Southwestern Furnishings, Inc., 4024 Montana Ave., El Paso, TX 79902; (877) 455-1455 (toll-free), or (915) 566-2025. Lots of chunky wood furniture, plus decorating accessories.

INTERIOR DESIGN

Clay and Colvin Design, 2345 West Mockingbird, Ste. 4, Dallas, TX 75235; (214) 350-7099. Mark Clay, principal. Interior design with a focus on traditional interiors, including ranches, country, Southwest, English, French, modern. International clientele.

POTTERY

True West, RR2 Goldthwaite, TX 76844; (915) 948-3768. "Rodeo Pattern," first produced in the 1940s by Wallace China Co., is still being made in the U.S.A. The original heavy roll rim design and colors are so accurate you can mix it with your old china. Dishwasher and microwave safe.

Colorado

FURNITURE AND ACCESSORIES

Four Winds (Furniture and accessories from all directions), 919 Main Ave., Durango, CO 81301; (970) 247-3701; www.elbertcreek.com. Unique mountain furnishings.

Jackalope, 12450 South Parker Rd., Parker, CO 80134; (303) 805-7687; www.Jackalope.com. Casual home furnishings and primitives from around the world.

Mesa Verde Pottery and Gallery Southwest, 27601 Hwy 160 East, Cortez, CO, 81321; 1-800-441-9908.

Notah Dineh Trading Co. and Museum, 345 W. Main, Cortez, CO 81321; 1-800-444-2024. Navajo rugs, jewelry, sand paintings, kachinas, and more.

New Mexico

BATH FIXTURES

Rainbow Gate, 530 S. Guadalupe St., Santa Fe, NM 87501; (505) 983-8892. Quality ceramic sinks in the Spanish tradition.

CABINETS

Cabinets Southwest, 321 E. Historic 66th, Church Rock, NM 87311; (505) 726-0826. Custom and modular cabinets for kitchen and bath.

CERAMIC AND QUARRY TILE

Arius Tiles, 12 miles north of Santa Fe on highway 84/285 in Pojoaque, NM. Also, PO Box 3767, Santa Fe, NM 87501; (505) 455-7466, (888) 455-7466. Custom handmade tile in a wide range of specialized and unique colors and designs. Open showroom.

Artesanos Imports Co., 1414 Maclovia St., Santa Fe, NM 87501; (505) 471-8020; http://www.artesanos.com. A full range of Southwestern tiles—Talavera, Saltillo quarry tile, ceramics in various colors and motifs.

Saltillo Tile Co., 851 San Mateo #8, Santa Fe, NM 87505; (505) 820-1830. In Albuquerque, 2601 Vassar NE, Albuquerque, NM 87107; (505) 881-8669. A complete range of glazed tiles, ribbons, liners, and ropes in any style or color. Talavera, quarry, and plain tiles available.

Tiles de Santa Fe, Inc., PO Box 3767, Santa Fe, NM 87501-0767; (505) 455-7466; www.tilesdesantafe.com. Handmade floor and wall tile for interiors and exteriors.

DESIGNERS

Jane Smith Interiors, 550 Canyon Rd., Santa Fe, NM 87501; (505) 988-4775.

Little & Trowbridge Design Studio, 213 East Marcy St., Santa Fe, NM 87501; (505) 995-8214.

Martin Kuckly, 5 Basin View, Santa Fe, NM 87501; (505) 983-4489.

Susan Dupepe Interior Design & Associates, 220 Mckenzie St., Santa Fe, NM 87501; (505) 982-4536.

T. C. Donobedian Interior Design, 203 East Palace Ave., Santa Fe, NM 87501; (505) 989-7405.

Wiseman & Gale & Duncan Interiors, 150 S. St. Francis Dr., Santa Fe, NM 87501; (505) 984-8544.

DOORS AND GATES

La Puerta, Inc., 1302 Cerrillos Rd., Santa Fe, NM 87501; (800) 984-8164; www.lapuertainc.com. Custom furniture from reclaimed wood, wooden doors and gates. Also buys doors and gates as is.

Spanish Pueblo Doors, 1091 Siler Rd., Unit B-1, PO Box 2517, Santa Fe, NM 87504-2517; (505) 473-0464, fax (505)473-1750. Solid wood doors in weathered textures and antique finishes.

FURNITURE AND ACCESSORIES

American Country Collection, 620 Cerrillos Rd., Santa Fe, NM 87501; (505) 984-0955. European antique furniture, rugs, fabrics, and leather furniture.

Ann Lawrence Antiques, 805 Early St., Santa Fe, NM 87501; (505) 984-1159. Textiles and heirloom linens, lace, furniture, majolica and collectibles.

Antiques on Grant, 136 Grant Ave., Santa Fe, NM 87501; (505) 995-9701. Eight dealers featuring furniture, textiles, folk art, porcelain, and fine art.

Antique Warehouse, 530 S. Guadalupe, Santa Fe, NM 87501; (505) 984-1159. Unique selection of Mexican doors, ranch furniture, and Spanish Colonial antiques.

Casa Bonita, 1900 Avenida de Mesilla, Las Cruces, NM; (505) 525-0449. Huge selection of terra cotta and concrete pottery, statuary, sun faces, decorative steel, Southwestern rugs, Mexican crafts, and chile ristras.

Conlon Siegal Galleries, 702 & 702 1/2 Canyon Rd., Santa Fe, NM 87501; (505) 820-3300. Specializing in ancient textiles from South America, Africa, Indonesia, and China.

Coyote Traders, 1020 West Picacho, Las Cruces, NM 88005; (505) 523-1284. Furniture and decorating items in wood and metal.

El Paso Import Co., 3500 Central SE, Albuquerque, NM; (505) 265-1160; Fax (505) 265-1274. In Santa Fe, 419 Sandoval Street, Santa Fe, NM 87501; (505) 982-5698, fax (505) 983-1522. Quality primitives and reproductions from the Mexican countryside.

Four Winds, 901 Canyon Rd., Santa Fe, NM 87501; (505) 982-1494, (505) 820-2971. Fine country furniture and primitives from around the world.

Foxglove Antiques, 260 Hyde Park Rd., Santa Fe, NM; (505) 986-8285. European country antiques.

Jackalope, 2820 Cerrillos Rd., Santa Fe, NM 87505; (505) 471-8539, (800) 753-7757. In Bernalillo, 834 Highway 44 (at the Rio Grande), Bernalillo, NM 87004; (505) 867-9813; www.Jackalope.com. Corporate office and designer showroom in Albuquerque, 8520 Pan American Highway NE, Ste. E; (505) 821-6500. Casual home furnishings and primitives from around the world.

Main Street Antique Mall, 2301 S. Main St., Las Cruces, NM 88005; (505) 523-0047. Open seven days a week with more than 40 dealers.

Marc Navarro Gallery, 822 Canyon Rd., Santa Fe, NM 87501; (505) 986-8191. Antique Latin American silver and jewelry. Specializes in devotional art.

Mary Corley Antiques, 215 N. Guadalupe, Santa Fe, NM 87501; (505) 984-0863. French, Spanish, Italian and English country antiques.

Mesilla Woodworks, 1802 Avenida De Mesilla, Las Cruces, NM 88005; (505) 523-1362. Handcrafted Southwest style furniture made to order or off the floor.

Morning Star Gallery, 513 Canyon Rd., Santa Fe, NM 87501; (505) 982-8187. Masterpieces of antique American Indian art.

Nomads, 207 Shelby St., Santa Fe, NM 87501; (505) 986-0855, (800) 360-4807. Specializing in tribal art, antique pottery, ethnic jewelry, primitive kilims, and architectural artifacts (doors, windows, and grilles) imported direct from Afghanistan, India, and North Africa, primarily Morocco.

Old Town Albuquerque, the original center of the city, a good place to view old architecture amid a myriad of courtyards, cobblestones, galleries, shops and restaurants, offering a blend of traditional and contemporary Indian, Western, Spanish and Mexican crafts.

Ortega's Weaving Shop, PO Box 325, Chimayó, New Mexico 87522; (505) 351-4215; (877) 3514215; www.ortegasdechimayo.com. Genuine, traditional, handwoven, 100% wool Chimayó rugs, blankets, garments, and accessories.

Peyton Wright, 237 East Palace Ave., Santa Fe, NM 87501; (505) 989-9888, (800) 879-8898. Ethnographic and Spanish Colonial art and antiquities.

Ron Messick Fine Arts, 1600 Canyon Rd., Santa Fe, NM 87501; (505) 983-9533. Pre-Columbian artifacts, South American and Continental antiques and paintings.

Santa Fe Pottery, 323 S. Guadalupe St., Santa Fe, NM 87501; (505) 989-3363; e-mail: SFPottery@roadrunner.com. Santa Fe's premier collection of regional contemporary crafts—ceramics, dinnerware, wood, glass, jewelry, lamps and lighting fixtures; including Santa Fe's oldest lighting company, Santa Fe Lights.

Santa Kilim, 401 S. Guadalupe, Santa Fe, NM 87501; (505) 986-0340. Fine tribal rugs, kilims and dhurries, plus upholstered furniture, primitive architectural pieces, and pottery.

Seret & Sons, 224 Galisteo, Santa Fe, NM 87501; (505) 988-9151. Furniture and rugs from the Middle and Far East, including Tibeten trunks and cabinets. All furniture is antique and/or unique one-of-a-kind pieces.

Southwest Spanish Craftsmen, 328 Guadalupe, P.O. Box 1805, Santa Fe, NM 87504; (505) 982-1767; (800) 777-1767; Fax (505) 982-7300. Over 70 years of handcrafting one-of-a-kind furniture.

Strictly Southwestern, Inc., 1321 Eubank NE, Albuquerque, NM 07112; (505) 292-7337. Large warehouse filled with lighting and furniture.

Susan Tarman Antiques and Fine Art, 923 Paseo de Peralta, Santa Fe, NM 87501; (505) 983-2336. Seventeenth through nineteenth century American, Oriental, and European furniture, porcelain and silver.

T. C. Donobedian's Paris Flea, 203-209 East Palace, Santa Fe, NM 87501; (505) 989-7405. Variety of French flea market finds, mid- to early-twentieth century Continental furniture, lanterns, and light fixtures, rugs, and more.

Taos Furniture, 1807 2nd St. Suite #100, Santa Fe, NM 87505; (505) 988-1229, (800) 443-3448; www.taosfurniture.com. Manufacturer of high-end Southwestern furniture. All pieces are hand planed and available in all types of styles.

The Design Center, 418 Cerrillos Rd., Santa Fe, NM 87501; Harry Greiner Antiques (505) 820-7094; Gloria List Gallery (505) 982-5622; Alex Abel antiques (505) 986-8728; Claiborne Gallery (505) 982-8019. Large array of antiques and furnishings ranging from Continental, Spanish and South American colonial to Art Deco.

Tierra Wools, 91 Main St., Los Ojos, New Mexico 87551; (505) 588-7231 or (888) 709-0979. Handwoven natural dyed rugs and blankets inspired by Rio Grande designs.

Wiseman & Gale & Duncan Interiors, 150 S. St. Francis Dr., Santa Fe, NM 87501; (505) 984-8544. Antiques, fabrics, and home furnishings.

HARDWARE

Old World Hardware, 621 Santa Fe Trail, Santa Fe, NM 87501; (505) 983-3566. Representing over 20 blacksmiths who handcraft and handforge pieces of hardware. Door hardware and lighting fixtures also available.

IRONWORKS

Christopher Thomson Ironworks, PO Box 578, Ribera, NM 87560; (505) 421-2645, (800) 726-0145. Custom-designed hardware and ironwork.

LIGHTING

Southwestern Lights, PO Box 548, Santa Fe, NM 87504-0548; (505) 473-1077. Custom-made pottery lights with Southwestern motifs in natural shades—sconces, lanterns, chandeliers.

TINWORK

Richard J. Fisher Tinwork, #9 Griegos Arroyo Rd., Tesuque, NM; (505) 989-4227. Custom-made, one-of-a-kind tinwork.

WINDOWS

Pozzi Wood Windows, 2774 Aqua Fria, Ste. B-1, Santa Fe, NM 87505; (505) 473-0554. Quality wood windows in historic and contemporary Southwest styles.

Arizona

FURNITURE AND ACCESSORIES

Antigua de Mexico, 7037 N. Oracle Rd., Tucson, AZ 85704; (520) 742-7114. Custom Mexican colonial furniture, wrought iron, folk art, glassware, ceramics, tinware, lighting.

Bates Architectural Collection, 4238 N. Craftsman Ct., Scottsdale, AZ 85251; (480) 970-3025; www.batesarchitectural.com. Collection of antiquities, santos, alters, furniture (most 200 to 400 years old) from Mexico and Guatemala.

Casa Decor, 7415 W. Boston and Chandler, Phoenix, AZ 85226; (480) 785-2001. Ten thousand-square-foot warehouse full of rustic Mexican-style furniture and accessories.

El Paso Imports, Camelback and 16th Street, 4750 N. 16th Street, Phoenix, AZ 85016; (602) 222-9932, Fax (602) 222-9208. In Tucson, 3550 N. Oracle Rd. Ste. 15, Tucson, AZ 85705; (520) 293-2614. Quality primitives and reproductions from the Mexican countryside.

Esperanza, 10685 N. 69th St., Scottsdale, AZ 85254; (480) 922-9130. In Albuquerque, 303 Grande Rio Blvd. NW, Albuquerque, NM 87104; (505) 242-6458. Custom handcrafted Southwestern furniture available in 18 finishes and several fabric choices.

Holler and Saunders Ltd., P.O. Box 2151, Nogales, AZ 85628-2151; (505) 287-5153. Antique and contemporary furniture, stone, pottery, decorative arts.

Kaibab Courtyard Shops, 2837-41 North Campbell Ave., Tucson, AZ 85719; (520) 795-6905. Fine old Mexican furniture, large Talavera selection, baskets, Mexican folk art, Navajo weavings, and Pueblo pottery.

Lost Barrio Warehouse Shopping District, Park Avenue just south of Broadway. Tucson's premier interior design resource concentrating on Southwestern and ethnic styles in furniture, accessories, primitive and tribal artifacts, architectural elements, garden ornaments, functional and fine arts.

Old Town Artisans, 201 N. Court Ave., Tucson, AZ 85701; (520) 623-6024, (800) 782-8072. A historic adobe marketplace featuring one-of-a-kind work by area artisans, tucked away in the city's oldest historic district. Some furniture, household accents.

Sonoran Designs, 2901 E. Broadway Blvd, Tucson, AZ; (520) 320-3916. Unique handcrafted metal furniture and accessories.

Southwest Interiors, 3766 East Grant Rd., Tucson, AZ; (520) 881-2210. Furniture and decorating items.

Timeless Treasures, Copper Queen Plaza, Bisbee, AZ; (520) 432-5888. Large collection of antiquities of the American West, including mining and cowboy paraphernalia.

Work of Artists Gallery, 10835 N. Tatum Blvd., Ste. 101, Phoenix, AZ 85028; (480) 596-0304. Over 200 Arizona artists in many media—sculpture, paintings, furniture, photography, metalworks, and more.

World of Rugs, 8989 E. Indian Bend, Rd., Scottsdale, AZ 85250; (602) 998-4108. In Phoenix, 13637 N. Tatum Blvd., Phoenix, AZ 85032, (602) 953-3238, as well as other Arizona locations.

DESIGNERS
Wiseman & Gale Interiors Inc., 4015 North Marshall Way, Scottsdale, AZ 85251; (480) 945-8447, fax (480) 423-5043.

TILE
Mexican Tile Company, 2222 E. Thomas Rd., Phoenix, AZ 85016, (602) 954-6271. In Tucson, 148 E. Broadway, Tuscon, AZ 85719, (520) 622-4320. Imported Mexican tiles, pavers, roof tiles, and natural stone.

National Sources
BLANKETS & PILLOWS
Pendleton Woolen Mills, PO Box 3030, Portland, OR 97201-3030; (503) 226-4801. Contact the manager of the blanket division for a list of stores near you.

GreenHome.com, (877) 282-6400; www.greenhome.com.

FIREPLACES
Heatilator, 1915 West Saunders St., Mt. Pleasant, IA 52641; (800) 843-2848, (319) 385-9211; http://www.heatilator.com. Both gas and wood fireplaces.

LIGHTING
Arroyo Craftsman, 2880 B Central Ave., Duarte, CA 91010; (818) 359-3298. Interior and exterior lighting in the Craftsman style.

GreenHome.com, (877) 282-6400; www.greenhome.com.

PAINT
Aura Natural Paints, Sinan, PO Box 857, Davis, CA 95617; (916) 753-3104; www.dcn.davis.ca.us/go/sinan. An eco-friendly alternative to commercial paints.

Earthues, 5129 Ballard Ave. NW, Seattle, WA 98107; (206) 789-1065. A natural dye company.

Nontoxica, (800) 731-5007; www.nontoxica.com. Safe, durable, VOC-free, odorless paints.

GreenHome.com, (877) 282-6400; www.greenhome.com.

Ralph Lauren suede paint, Quality deep-hued paint with texture sold through the national chain of Lowes stores.

Weathermax, (800) 920-9969; http://primeshop.com. High-tech wood sealant/stain. No VOCs, nontoxic, environmentally friendly.

Wellborn Paints, 215 Rossmoor Rd. SW, Albuquerque, NM 87102; (800) 432-4069. Full line of paints and stains sold exclusively in the Southwest.

RAMMED-EARTH CONSTRUCTION
Information available on the web at www.rammedearth.com.

WINDOWS
Pozzi Wood Windows, 2774 Aqua Fria, Ste. B-1, Santa Fe, NM 87505; (505) 473-0554. Quality wood windows in historical and contemporary Southwest styles.

Glossary

Adobe: Earth mixed with water and straw, then either poured into forms or made into sun-dried bricks. See "Terrone adobe."

Adz: A hatchetlike tool with a flat blade head that leaves a distinctive, rough surface. Used to remove bark from heavy timbers in forming vigas and latillas.

Alacena: A large cupboard built into the thick adobe walls of Spanish Colonial houses.

Armoire: French; an upright cabinet used as a wardrobe.

Balloon framing: A building method that distributes structural loads to each of a series of relatively lightweight studs.

Baluster: An upright support for a rail in a staircase, balcony, etc.

Bulto: Carved and painted representation of a saint, usually three dimensional.

Buttes: See "Mesas and Buttes."

Caja: Large trunk in the Spanish Colonial tradition.

Canale: Water spout in old adobe construction, used to carry rain and melting snow off flat roofs to the ground.

Carpentiro: Spanish carpenter.

Casa: Spanish; house.

Casita: Spanish; small house.

Chimayó: An old American Indian/Spanish settlement twenty-five miles north of Santa Fe, New Mexico, with a rich tradition in Rio Grande weaving.

Chip-carving: Technique used to carve designs into furniture using a hammer and a variety of chisels to achieve a bas-relief effect.

Concha: Shell-shaped ornamentation.

Coping: A finishing or protective course or cap to an exterior masonry or adobe wall.

Corbel: A short, horizontal timber used for support; sometimes carved or otherwise decorated.

Cornice: Horizontal member that crowns a composition or facade.

Creosote: An evergreen shrub of the desert Southwest. One of the oldest known living plants.

Dado: The lower part of a wall when specially decorated.

Dentil: A small rectangular block in a series projecting from a wall like teeth, as under a cornice.

Distressing: A finishing technique that became popular in the 1980s in which wood is stained, scratched, sandblasted, beaten with chains, or any other inventive technique designed to "distress" the surface and make it look old.

Door Panels: Door surfaces allowing artistic expression by crafts-people. Southwestern panels are often carved, inset with punched tin, painted, or built up with applied moldings.

Dovetail joints: Carpentry term. A joint formed of one or more tenons (that are broader at the end than at the base) fitting tightly within corresponding mortises.

Drywall: An interior building material consisting of sheets of gypsum that are faced with heavy paper on both sides. Also known as gypsum board and plaster board.

Equipale: Pigskin and cedar furniture from Jalisco, Mexico, which dates to the 1500s.

Footprint: The size of a structure's imprint on the land on which it stands, like the print of a foot is to a human.

Four Corners: The only place in the United States where four states meet—Arizona, Utah, New Mexico, and Colorado. Two American Indian reservations (Navajo and Ute) also abut each other at this point.

Galeria: A gallery in a Spanish Colonial–style house, usually serving as the main entrance to the house.

Glazing: The process of installing glass by securing it with glazier's points and glazing compound.

Greek Revival: An architectural style characterized by formal symmetry, pediments, dentils, and wood molding. Floor plan is centered around a central hall and entry.

Hacienda: Large manor house in the Spanish Colonial–style, single rooms aligned horizontally, the entire structure shaped in a square built around a central courtyard.

Hardware: Locks, hinges, drawer pulls, and other functional metal parts of furniture. Often made of wrought iron, Southwestern hardware also incorporates bone, tin, copper, even leather straps.

Harinero: Large Spanish grain chest.

Hogan: The traditional housing of the Navajo, a conical eight-sided house usually made of logs and covered with earth with a smoke hole at the top. Usually entered through a short, covered passage.

Horno: An Arabic-influenced beehive adobe oven used to bake bread outdoors.

Jerga: A handwoven rug made of coarse homespun wool in the Spanish/Mexican tradition.

Joinery: The technique of joining two or more pieces of wood with a mortise-and-tenon, dovetail, rabbet, or dado.

Kachinas: The pantheon of intermediaries to the gods in the spirit world of Hopi and Zuni cultures. Kachina dolls are meant as learning aids, not playthings.

Kiva: Hopi word for ceremonial room. Underground chambers, usually entered from a ladder at the top, designed for meetings and worship of family clans of the Pueblo people. Can be compared to churches of modern times.

Latilla: Poles, usually pine or aspen, placed side by side on top of vigas in adobe-style houses; or one of a series of poles used in a fence.

Lintel: A load-bearing beam over an opening, such as a door or window.

Loggia: An indoor/outdoor space open to the air on at least one side, usually the ceiling.

Mesas and buttes: Different shapes of elevated landmasses composed of soft rock and therefore susceptible to erosion. A flat-topped rock is called a "mesa," the Spanish word for "table." If the rock has eroded to the point where it is no longer wider than it is tall, it is called a "butte." Further erosion narrows a butte to a degree where it is called a "monument," "pinnacle," or "spire."

Metate: A flat stone containing a shallow depression for holding maize or other grains to be ground.

Milagros: Small tin representations of animals or parts of the body that are pinned with prayers to the robes of carved saints in churches throughout Mexico and Central America.

Mission: A colonization strategy employed by the Spanish centering on a church, dormitories, stables, gardens, and other necessities of survival on the frontier. New Mexico, Arizona, Texas, and California have preserved mission complexes.

Moors: Members of the Muslim population of Spain, of mixed Arab, Spanish, and Berber origins; subsequently settled in North Africa between the eleventh and seventeenth centuries.

Mortise-and-tenon: A wood joint with one end shaped into a male rectangular peg (tenon) designed to fit into a square socket (mortise). Tenon ends may be concealed, exposed, or extended beyond the joint frame. The joint is commonly pegged for stability.

Muntin: A vertical bar in a window sash.

Nicho: Small niche carved into an adobe wall.

Oratorio: A chapel or altar used for meditation and prayer.

Padercita: Small wall, usually stepped.

Parapet: A low wall or railing on a flat roof.

Paredcito: Small, low kneewall forming one wall of a corner fireplace.

Pediment: Decoration over portico, doorway, or window; usually in the Greek Revival style.

Pedestrian door: A small hinged door built within a much larger gate. Where the gate is large enough for carriages and ox carts to enter, the smaller door allows easier passage for people.

Penasco: A unique folk style characterized by innovative uses of decorative molding and raised and recessed panels. Named after a New Mexican mountain village. Used for doors and furniture.

Petroglyph: Design carved into rock.

Pictograph: Painted design on rock.

Pintle hinge: A wooden hinge Spanish settlers made to hang doors. It's actually a carved protrusion extending from the same wood as the door and fits into holes in the door frame so the door swings on it.

Placita: Fortified place, small town, court, or patio.

Plaza: The central area in a town, town square.

Portal: A long, deep one-story covered porch used to shield the house from direct southwest sun. Usually supported by posts and corbels (often decorated) and found especially in Territorial-style houses.

Post-and-beam: A basic building method that uses a few hefty posts and beams to support an entire structure.

Presidio: Fortified outposts, generally in Arizona, established by Spanish explorers to protect nearby missions, ranches, and mines from Indian attack.

Puddled adobe: Method of building with mud in which layers are built up slowly, directly on the wall, and left to dry between courses.

Pueblo: A solid structure of adobe brick or stone set in clay and mortar. Rooms are square with thick, flat roofs built in terraced stories. Access to interiors is by ladders to trapdoors in the roofs. Outer walls have neither windows nor doors as a precaution against attackers.

R-value: Measurement of a material's resistance in transmitting heat. The higher the R-value, the more energy efficient a product is.

Ramada: An open shelter, often with a thatched roof.

Rammed earth: A method of constructing earth walls by placing moistened soil into forms and ramming it into place, after which the forms are removed.

Reredos: Simple scenes painted on planks of wood and used as altar screens in Spanish Mission churches.

Retablo: A two-dimensional painting of a saint or holy person, usually on a flat board. Desirable as folk art.

Ropero: Spanish for armoire.

Rout: To shape edges or cut grooves using a router.

Saguaro: Large cactus, native to the Sonoran Desert.

Sala: Living room, or main room in the Spanish Colonial tradition.

Sanefa: Painted border, stripe, or stencil on the bottom part of a wall.

Santo: Image or statue of a saint.

Santuario: A small sanctuary, usually belonging to a home.

Sash: Framework of a window in which panes of glass are set.

Sipapu or Sipapuni: A hole in the floor in kivas and pit houses (in the Anasazi tradition); symbolic entrance to the underworld.

Tabla: Rough-hewn roof planking.

Talavera tile: Interlocking ceramic tiles in Moorish designs made in Puebla, Mexico. They come in a variety of colors and glazes and are particularly desirable in kitchens and baths.

Territorial: A hybrid Greek Revival- and American-style house characterized by a symmetrical center hall plan, and brick coping; developed in the Southwest after 1820.

Terrone adobe: Old way of building adobe houses in northern New Mexico. Hispanic people carved mud blocks from the riverbank and hauled them back to the site to use as building blocks. A network of root and organic matter made the blocks strong and stable.

Thermopane: Vacuum-sealed insulating window, usually double or triple glazed.

Tongue-and-groove joint: A joint made using boards that have a projecting tongue on the end of one member and a corresponding groove on the other member into which the tongue fits.

Trastero: A large upright cabinet or cupboard often showcasing fine carpentry skills and designs.

Travertine: Marble that is a limestone composite.

Trombe wall: A wall built of thermal mass designed to store the sun's heat and slowly release it at night or on cloudy days.

Verde: Spanish; green.

Viga: Large timbers used in a framework for horizontal ceiling beams.

Wainscot: Lower three or four feet of a wall when finished differently from the rest of the wall.

Wattle and daub: A vertical framework of woven twigs and thin poles on which mud is plastered.

Záguan: Covered entrance between the outside and an enclosed courtyard, indicative of Spanish Colonial fortress architecture.

Zambullo: A simple window in the Spanish Colonial tradition made entirely of wood without metal hinges.

Zapata: Elegant corbel in the Spanish tradition.

Bibliography

Abbey, Edward. "Poetic Landscape." In *The Journey Home.* New York: Penguin Books USA, Inc., 1977.

Alexander, Christopher. *A Pattern Language.* Oxford University Press, 1977.

Arden, Harvey. *Noble Red Man: Lakota Wisdomkeeper Mathew King.* Hillsboro, OR: Beyond Words Publishing, 1994.

Baca, Elmo and Suzanne Deats. *Santa Fe Fantasy.* Santa Fe: Clear Light Publishing, 1994.

Baker, John Milnes AIA. *American House Styles: A Concise Guide.* New York: W.W. Norton & Co., 1994.

Becker, Ellie. "Remembering Betty." *Santa Fe Real Estate Weekly,* May 20, 1994.

Caldwell, E.K. "Relinquishing a Legacy of Hatred, Embracing Respect for All Life: Conversations with Dino Butler." *News From Indian Country.* (Five-part series), 1995.

Cather, Willa. *Death Comes For The Archibishop.* New York: Alfred A. Knopf, 1927.

Chesterfield, Mary. "Sitting on a Gold Mine." *Phoenix Home & Garden,* Oct. 1995.

Dennis, Landt and Lisl. *Behind Adobe Walls.* San Francisco: Chronicle Books, 1997.

Eastman, Charles Alexander. *The Soul of the Indian.* Lincoln: University of Nebraska Press, 1911.

Francaviglia, Richard and Narratt, David, eds. *Essays on the Changing Images of the Southwest.* Arlington: University of Texas, 1994.

Glover, Wayne. *Kokopelli: Ancient Myth/Modern Icon.* Bellemont, AZ: Camelback/Canyonlands Publishing, 1995.

Kaplan, Robert D. *An Empire Wilderness: Travels Into America's Future.* New York: Random House, 1998.

Lamb, Susan. *Pueblo and Mission: Cultural Roots of the Southwest.* Flagstaff, AZ: Northland Publishing, 1997.

Mangum, Richard and Sherry. *One Woman's West.* Flagstaff, AZ: Northland Publishing, 1997.

Mather, Christine and Sharon Woods. *Santa Fe Style.* New York: Rizzoli, 1986.

Nerburn, Kent, ed. *The Wisdom of the Native Americans.* Novato, CA: New World Library, 1999.

Seth, Sandra and Laurel. *Adobe! Homes and Interiors of Taos, Santa Fe, and the Southwest.* Stamford, CT: Architectual Book Publishing Co., 1988.

Shi, David E. *In Search of the Simple Life.* Salt Lake City: Perengrine Smith Books, 1986.

Silverbird, J. Reuben. *The World In Our Eyes.* compact disc; Tucson, AZ: Celestrial Harmonies, 1991.

Spears, Beverly. *American Adobe: Rural Houses of Northern New Mexico.* Albuquerque: University of New Mexico Press, 1986.

Stickley, Gustav. *Craftsman Homes: Architecture and Furnishings of the American Arts and Crafts Movement.* New York: Dover Publications, Inc., 1979.

The Comanche (Texas) Chief, 19 August 1937, 18 June 1987, 9–16 July 1987, 15 June 1989.

Varney, Philip. *Arizona Ghost Towns and Mining Camps.* Phoenix, AZ: Arizona Highways, 1994.

Wallis, Michael. *Route 66: The Mother Road.* New York: St. Martin's Press, 1990.

Warren, Nancy Hunter. *New Mexico Style: A Sourcebook of Traditional Architectural Details.* Santa Fe: Museum of New Mexico Press, 1986.

Acknowledgments

First and foremost, a heartfelt thank you to all the homeowners who graciously allowed us into their homes. Without them, and their expert style, there would be no book.

Also thank you to Lisa Newsom, since many of these photographs first appeared in *Veranda* magazine.

Thanks to Jeffrey Cook, Regents' Professor of Architecture at Arizona State University, for information about Southwest architectural styles; and to architect Bennie Gonzales for setting me straight on the historic architecture of Arizona.

Thank you to Margaret Waring, who undertook the chore of researching the history behind Mark Clay's delightful cottage in Comanche, Texas.

A hearty thanks to Shirley Isgar and David Alford who let me hang out at the Blue Lake Ranch near Durango, Colorado, eat their fresh home-cooked food, play my flute, study the mountains, and absorb the culture by osmosis.

Thanks to Pendleton Woolen Mills for use of colorful woolen blankets as props.

Special, special thank you to Carol Anthony, for a delicious, memorable morning in her cloister. From one old soul to another, I honor and salute you.

A humble thanks to Noël Bennett, for riding out our collaboration to a fruitful end.

Thanks to Edie Blackstone for her energy and perseverance.

Thanks to Stephanie Bucholz, my trustworthy editor, and to Kim Fox, research assistant at Northland, for digging deep and persevering to get me what I want when I want it.

Many, many thanks from the heart to Vanessa "Ann" Holtz, my valued and able editorial assistant, for her cheerful manner, prompt delivery, adept organizational skills, reliable friendship, and adventurous spirit. We see differently but with the same eyes.

A humble thank you to Peter Vitale for his superb magic with the camera.

And, of course, always and forever a quiet thank you to my driver and partner, Robert Chappell, for his support and patient understanding, and for at least pretending to listen throughout the seven months of labor it took to birth this book.

Index